Back in the Day

MY LIFE AND TIMES WITH TUPAC SHAKUR

Back in the Day

MY LIFE AND TIMES WITH TUPAC SHAKUR

DARRIN KEITH BASTFIELD

One World • Ballantine Books • New York

B
SHA
BAS

A One World Book
Published by The Ballantine Publishing Group

Copyright © 2002 by Born Busy Productions, Inc.

All rights reserved under International and Pan-American Copyright Conventions.
Published in the United States by The Ballantine Publishing Group,
a division of Random House, Inc., New York, and simultaneously in
Canada by Random House of Canada Limited, Toronto.

One World and Ballantine are registered trademarks and the One World
colophon is a trademark of Random House, Inc.

www.ballantinebooks.com/one/

Library of Congress Cataloging-in-Publication Data is available upon request from the
publisher.

ISBN 0-345-44775-1

Manufactured in the United States of America

First Edition: June 2002

10 9 8 7 6 5 4 3 2 1

I dedicate this book to these black men who have been an inspiration to the world. I don't feel that any structured order for the following names is necessary, for they are, as we all are, the embodiment of one collective soul—the universal soul.

Imhotep
Paul Robeson
Marcus Garvey
Martin Luther King Jr.
El Hajj Malik El-Shabazz
Reginald Lewis
Miles Davis
Jimi Hendrix
Redd Foxx
Richard Pryor
Dick Gregory
Bill Cosby
Elijah Muhammad
Quincy Jones
James Brown
Muhammad Ali
Stevie Wonder
Dr. Henry Clark
Dr. Yusef Ben Jochannan

Prince
Melvin Van Peebles
Sammy Davis Jr.
Michael Jackson
Jesse Jackson
Spike Lee
Magic Johnson
Marvin Gaye
Alex Haley
Earth, Wind and Fire
Russell Simmons
Run-DMC
Les Brown
Bob Marley
Dr. Cheikh Anta Diop
James Baldwin
Michael Jordan
W.E.B. DuBois
Frederick Douglass

THIS TESTAMENT

You paved these streets leaving intense memories of footprints
With every stride on ground you traveled in hope to avoid nonsense
Your energy rang a perfect pitch holding aside your wounds life
    bitched
Then noted your lessons of preparation from those cuts unstitched
Was it a coincidence? I asked. Your foretelling words were kept
Not arbitrarily, once realized your words and destiny soon met
You knew that fate would not have waited through its total control
So no fear of death strengthened you whole to be willing and able
    to let go
This testament I write embraces words of my truest intent
To shed pure light and cast a shadow on ones laced with false pretense
I strongly feel that you're with us as part of your path I tell
At last, you yelled your struggle, and gave us guide of how one's
    soul propels

BY DARRIN KEITH BASTFIELD

"I honestly didn't care whether I lived or died.
But now I cannot die with people thinkin' I'm a rapist or a criminal.
I can't leave 'til this shit is straight.
I'm not suicidal; I can't go 'til y'all know what time it is."

TUPAC AMARU SHAKUR
MTV INTERVIEW, 1995

Contents

Acknowledgments

I would like to thank my brilliant editor, Anita Diggs, of One World/ Ballantine Books for seeing the vision, opening the door, and bringing out the best in me. You were born to do what you do!

I would also like to thank my wonderful agent, Wendy Sherman, for believing in my story, advising me, and bringing me to the world of the published author. I look forward to us having a lasting working relationship. You are a winner!

Having served an integral part in helping me tell my story, I want to thank Scott Carroll for his writing contributions. Thank you, Scott, for becoming absorbed with my efforts and sharing your creative energy by adding your brush strokes to canvas for the greater purpose of telling the truth. It wasn't easy, but no matter what, the ball kept rolling!

I would also like to extend my appreciation to the supportive and loving soul of my life, Lynda E. Evans, for her contributions in the development of this book.

I would like to thank Shawn Evans-Mitchell, professor of journalism at Clark Atlanta University; and Lawrence Jackson, professor of English at Howard University; for their in-depth constructive criticism. I enjoyed the honor of having such skilled sets of eyes and brilliant minds turn the pages of my manuscript.

I would like to thank my entire family, especially my mother, Barbara Jean Samuel, and my grandmother, Eva May Bastfield, for their support throughout my entire life.

I would like to thank those who have helped me along the way:

Morris Brown for advice at times I really needed it. Dana M. Smith, a.k.a. Mouse, you were there from the beginning of this journey and kept true in helping me shed a positive light on our friend. Gerard Young, my brother from way back, thank you for your support and coming through when you did. To Gerard's parents, my second parents, Mr. and Mrs. Young, for being positive influences in my younger years. Deborah Taylor, thank you for your generous support and sharing your memories with me. Giavanni Trunzo, my good friend, who has helped me in many ways throughout my time while living in California. Sean Robinson, thanks for encouraging me and pointing out what was really important—this book. Karen Lee, the music industry's most incredible publicist, thanks for your sincere insight and advice. You have been very dear to me. Thomas Dunaway, Ben and Hallie Flieshman, three who have been very supportive of me personally throughout my years in California. John Cole, it is good to know that we will always be friends in spirit. To Truxon M. Sykes, my spiritual mentor and good friend, you have opened my eyes wider to see the universe for what it truly embodies. I would also like to thank the Baltimore School for the Arts, Ms. Gladney, and my friends Alvin Petit, Tamara Payne, and Kendrick Sharpe.

I would like to thank those who have been supportive and have crossed over between the time I started and ended my journey of writing this book: Robert James Whittington, my cousin, who encouraged me to tell this story, and Robert O. Torrence, my mentor of Ma'at, father figure, and the greatest artist I have ever known.

I would like to give my respects to Tupac's family and extend my heartfelt appreciation to all the Tupac fans between Baltimore and California who shared with me your thoughts and questions. You all made it clear to me that this book was necessary.

Finally, I would like to thank the many legends of hip-hop for laying down the foundation of the ever-growing culture we all know today.

Prologue

When Tupac was asked as a young boy, "What do you want to be when you grow up?" his reply was, "a revolutionary." This piece of research I found particularly interesting among all else that I learned and remembered about him in my journey back in time because, in fact, Tupac was a revolutionary. He was an exceptional young man who saw a dire need for change, and he worked for this change with every breath that he took. Tupac's way was a provocative one. Forget all the nicety; he was as blunt as they come, and as bold. We often forget exactly how young he was, and the effect this would have on his approach to life. I believe Tupac was transitioning into a new, more sophisticated phase of his lifelong plan to bring about the above-mentioned change when, tragically, he was stopped short.

"What do you want to be when you grow up?" I'm quite sure everyone remembers being asked at some point in their childhood.

For most, "a revolutionary" was probably not among the list of possible responses. But Tupac was not like most. This little tale from Tupac's early childhood also struck me because I too had an unusual answer to this common childhood question; in fact it is the source of one of my earliest memories.

When I was four years old, in pre-k, the teacher was going around the circle of students seated on the carpet in the middle of the room. I remember many of the kids reciting the inevitable top three, "a fireman . . . a policeman . . . a doctor." It was strange because I knew what they were going to say before they said it. I remember sitting on the floor, looking into their unsure faces as they took their turn, while I contemplated whether I should also say, "fireman . . . policeman . . . doctor." I knew it would sound right if I did. And I all but convinced myself to do so as the teacher's gaze neared. Sure, I could say what was in my heart, but why be the outcast, the strange one, when this was so easily and harmlessly avoidable? Only six kids left and no one ventured the answer that was bouncing around in my head. "No, I'm just going to be like everybody else," I nervously decided as my turn approached. Then the kid directly before me admitted, "I don't know," smiling, like it was some kind of joke, or game.

What do you mean, you don't know?! You're in pre-k for God's sake! Get some direction in your life, you bum. Everybody else in here knows what they want to be! All these things raced through my thoughts, along with: *Thank you, now I'm not going to be the odd one after all.* My answer would be much better than his.

"I want to be a drawer," I proclaimed confidently when the teacher's eyes met mine. Most of the kids understood my answer. I was speaking in our language. Drawing was the usual pre-nap activity.

"No, Darrin, you mean artist, right?" the teacher suggested gently.

"No, drawer," was my steadfast reply. I had no idea what an artist was, and I didn't care. I just knew that I had a passion bigger than that of any other kid or adult I had ever met in my four years of life. As a child, I spent a great deal of time observing things, objects, people, and places. And I felt a burning need to record what I saw. The view out of my bedroom window, for instance, was of great importance to me—it was me, it was what I woke up to and went to sleep to everyday, so I drew a picture to show people, and always kept it folded in my pocket just in case.

My first drawing I remember clearly; it was of Fred Flintstone. I remember sitting in front of the television by myself studying him, trying to draw him exactly the way I saw him on the screen. Diligently, I watched day after day, paying close attention to the most minute details. I didn't want to miss a single thing. Every episode provided a new piece to the drawing, which I revisited for many days until I was satisfied. I knew it was good when people doubted that I was the true creator of the impressive replica. Most people I showed it to, mainly other children, thought I had traced it. That is, until I drew another, almost equally impressive rendering of Fred from memory, right in front of their faces. I had soaked him in. He was a part of my memory, ready and waiting to be regurgitated as often as I chose. And this was what everyone wanted! This elicited from them that response that was like food to my soul. From that point on I knew what I had to do: no big desire to change the world, no grand vision, just doing what came naturally, what made people want to take a minute of their time to look at the products of my hands, and the fruits of my mind.

I didn't know why I had this desire to observe and to draw. It just felt right. It wasn't until fourteen years later when I met my biological father and discovered that he too had this same passion, this same talent, that I understood. I had floated, unconsciously, purposelessly, through the gifted and talented program of my elementary school, the Baltimore School for the Arts, local and national art competitions, and a year at the School of Visual Arts in New York. Nothing had had any real meaning to me until I met my father. Now I know why it is important for me to draw pictures. It is a part of me. It is the reason why I simply had to take on this project.

Tupac was a genuinely intriguing subject on which I focused my sharpest attention from before our first encounter, and certainly afterward. We were alike in some ways, but in many more we were very different. Tupac was exceptional, on a grand scale, and I knew it. I watched him out of curiosity, but also in hope of borrowing some of whatever it was behind his strength, his drive, his propensity to excel in whatever direction he set his sights. Indeed, I watched him very closely. And upon his death, it became clear to me that it was time to draw the picture.

Throughout the effort behind this book, my goal has always been to show the world the real Tupac, the boy who grew into the man that lived and breathed behind the myth. My strategy for accomplishing this was simply to allow the reader a seat behind my eyes in the same room with him at his apartment, on the job at the restaurant where we worked, in the halls at school, at various parties, recording music into a little tape recorder, rehearsing rhymes, battling cats on the street, just hanging out listening to music, trippin' out on the back of the bus, etc. The list goes on. These are all simple things, the minute details that make the picture.

When Tupac began his rise to the top, I knew that the world was in for a big shock. I knew that people would not be able or willing to understand him. This was not based on some idea that he was crazy, or troubled, or even eccentric. It was based on my knowing him to be a deeply thoughtful artist whose puzzle had always been far too complicated for the average person to decipher in the insufficient amount of time the average person generally allots to art, popular or otherwise. For certain, I knew Tupac would not get sufficient consideration before his death. This society's inability to appreciate artists within the artist's lifetime is no big secret. But I've never been so shortsighted and so proud as to deny my fellow man his glory while he is yet beside me, in shoes just like mine, without the halo of death necessarily hoisting him high above. Many times I've returned to my old School for the Arts yearbook from 1988, where I wrote to Tupac on my farewell page: "Tupac, no one can stop you so never give them a chance. Soar to the top nonstop. Take it easy."

I was extremely fortunate to have been one of the people closest to Tupac in an important time in our development. My firsthand experience of him affected and continues to affect me profoundly. And it is my intention that all of you have this firsthand experience, and be duly affected by it.

# Introduction

On September 6, 1996, I heard the news that Tupac had been shot. Reacting to the shocking blurb scrolling across her pager, a female friend whom I was entertaining at my apartment in the area of Baltimore City known as Bolton Hill where Tupac had once lived more than eight years before, sounded confused and unsure. I convinced myself that she had gotten it wrong, that the message was in reference to the first shooting in New York in 1994; but this would not last for long. Listening to the radio we received the unsettling confirmation only moments later. I couldn't believe that he had been shot again. I felt helpless, forced to accept the possibility that this time he could die.

But he had been shot before, and had survived, I consoled myself. I felt sure that if he survived the first few days, as before, he would be all right. This I took for granted as time passed with no word of his death. But on the seventh day everything changed, the unthinkable transpired, Tupac was pronounced dead. The frustration I felt was as deep as the sadness.

For more than two months following the shooting, images of Tupac came to me in my dreams, riling me in my sleep, urging me to champion his story. But I wasn't sure if I could handle the responsibility. In fact, I seriously doubted myself. That's when the communications began to spill over beyond my dreams. Not only did thoughts of Tupac allow me no peaceful sleep, but he began to occupy my every waking thought, always there, night and day. I would awaken in the middle of the night, writing poetry and painting the vivid images from my dreams of him calling out to me. I asked another friend who had known Tupac to help me put together all of the pieces of our late friend's untold years in Baltimore in order to shed insight into his true character. He told me not to waste my time, and to move on, to concentrate on my own life because this wasn't worth the energy. Everyone, including a few in my own family, tried their best to discourage me, telling me that "others will have already done it." But I knew they didn't understand, that I knew a side of Tupac these "others" didn't even know existed, and that somehow Tupac was with me.

Relentlessly, I was haunted by this presence that wouldn't let me be. I could feel him everywhere. Broken and prepared to submit, I looked deeper for signs to further assure me that I was meant to write this book. The next day I received the first of many signs to come; strange coincidences, some would rather I say, but I know them as spiritual communications, or vibrations. It was at this point that my reluctance lifted and I pledged my full commitment to the story of this childhood friend who had meant so much to me. I didn't work a job. I devoted one hundred percent of my attention to the research and writing, employing all of my mental and physical energy to tell the truth.

Back in the Day
MY LIFE AND TIMES WITH TUPAC SHAKUR

His Name
Is What?!

"You can't stop me! / Not even your bad breath / You can't stop me! / 'Cuz my rhyme's so def / You can't stop me! / Not even when I'm calm / You couldn't stop me with a motherfuckin' nuclear bomb / You can't stop me!" These lyrics still echo in my mind, evoking visions of Tupac rapping in the hallways of the Baltimore School for the Arts with startling conviction. This is where I first met Tupac back in 1986. My best friend at the school and fellow visual artist, Gerard, told me of this new kid who was entering as a sophomore who was supposed to be a rapper. When he told me the kid's name was Tupac, I was like, "His name is what!?" He simply laughed and shook his head, confirming that I had heard him correctly. Gerard was familiar with the new kid's reputation as a rapper from his friends at Roland Park Middle, where he had graduated one year before Tupac's arrival in 1984. And his bus to and from the School for the Arts passed Roland Park on its way, so he had seen the new student several times wearing a T-shirt with MC NEW YORK written on it, rapping among his friends. A lot of guys were rapping at the time, so I wasn't overly impressed. But there was obviously something about this kid that had caught Gerard's attention.

The thought of a new rapper entering our ranks, particularly one whose reputation had preceded him, definitely sparked our curiosity, and probably our teenage insecurities. In our first two years at the school, Gerard and I, along with a number of other Black students (primarily guys), had dedicated a lot of time and effort to rapping. We were all driven young artists whose primary passions were for the talents that had won our admittance into the school. But as young Black inner-city boys in the mid-nineteen-eighties, we were drawn to rap, and the rapidly developing hip-hop culture in general. In the neighborhoods at the time, all of the boys and girls were listening to rap music. Although it was still underground in Baltimore, rap was almost the only music we were listening to. And many of us at the School for the Arts, already endowed with a definite artistic flair and creative disposition, were trying our hand at this popular new art form.

We regularly tested each other's lyrical ability in informal contests held mostly outside the school building on the sidewalks of Cathedral Street and Madison Avenue, the two thoroughfares bordering the school located on the corner of their intersection in downtown Baltimore. Admittedly, these contests were born from regular joke-cracking sessions, and maintained a lot of that feeling, focusing more on humor and insult than delivery, melody, and composition: the real measures of rap. Students with personal vendettas used this forum to attack each other as personally as they

could. Anything and everything was fair game. And whoever suc-
ceeded in embarrassing the other more was the victor. But steadily,
all of the jokesters were brushed aside and the rappers took center
stage. It was through the course of these impromptu sessions,
known as "The Dozens," that we established an informal hierarchy
among the rappers. And with this hierarchy we were beginning the
new year precisely where we had left off the previous spring. I was
anxiously awaiting the opportunity to assert myself anew and gain
new ground. I had written some new rhymes over the summer and
was ready. I suspected the same of a few peers but I knew I would
catch others sleepin'.

The most popular rapper was still Zorian, another name that always struck me as funny and odd. Zorian was a short, stocky, dark-
complected stage production student with thick eyeglasses who
always tried to hang with the brothers in the break-dancing crew.
But he didn't have the flavor or the skill, and they weren't impressed. So he concentrated on rapping, where, in all honesty, the
competition wasn't so intense. And he got to be pretty good, using
a lot of humor effectively in his rhymes. Although he had graduated
the previous spring, he was still around the school a lot, visiting
with friends and presiding over The Dozens. The primary members of the rap crew in the school were Zorian, Ernest, Kendrick,
and me. I was always a little closer to Zorian and Kendrick because
Ernest tended to have a lot of mouth, kind of a braggart who was
comfortable talking about people. Gerard was also part of the crew,
but he was more a DJ than a rapper. None of the various other contributors to our sessions presented any real challenge.

The arrival of the new rapper posed a problem. Where would he
fit in, if at all?, I wondered, before brushing aside the question. It

was not my problem. He was the new guy, and would have dues to pay. I could remember my first days at the school, the strange, mansionlike building with its polished marble stairway spiraling upward from the front foyer, the intimate studios, winding basement halls, and grand ballroom hovering dreamily within some plane of reality far removed from any school experience I had known, or even imagined: the shock, the touch of anxiety, the sheer newness. To become excited over the arrival of some greenhorn, some neophyte, would be ridiculous. Establishing one's self artistically in a student body so rich in talent spanning the full range of artistic pursuit was not easy. And regardless of the low buzz that had reached my ears, I knew it would not be easy for him.

I first noticed the new student walking down the marble front stairwell, talking with some of his classmates. He was dressed as if for church, with dark dress pants, a sweater over a dark dress shirt, and dress shoes. "Him?" I thought to myself as I looked at him through the door of my last-period sculpture class. Gerard and I shared this last-period class (really a studio) on Wednesdays and Fridays. And it was in this class that Gerard had been telling me more and more about the new kid every day. In fact he had just finished a Tupac story only minutes before.

The classroom was adjacent to the front foyer, with an outside door that opened on to the sidewalk on Madison Avenue, right in the middle of the throng of students gathering in the lobby and outside the front door everyday at four o'clock when everyone was dismissed for the day. Since students often stayed well after the end of school and into the evening to complete their assignments, teachers were not concerned with our taking frequent breaks and walking in and out of the studios, as long as we got our assignments done. So Gerard and I talked freely during this time in the studio, catching up on gossip and current events as we worked. And we frequently took part in the end-of-the-day commotion that erupted outside our classroom every day. It was at such a time, when virtually the entire student body was passing our room, that I saw Tupac walking down the spiral steps. I attempted to see before me the guy about whom I had heard so much, but I couldn't. This guy looked nothing like what I expected from all that I had been hearing.

Apparently, Tupac and Gerard lived on the same side of town (though Gerard was farther out, toward the county line) and caught the same bus to and from school. And according to Gerard, the seemingly quiet and guarded new kid blossomed into quite a different character once outside the school doors, serving as the life of the ride on most days. Gerard would always come to class with a new tale of Tupac antics from the back of the bus, unable to help but laugh as he relived the scene: "Man, he had us all dyin'," he would say. It was as if Tupac ran a regularly scheduled show every day, anticipated and even expected by all who would catch the bus. A lot of times Gerard would have a funny-ass rhyme to regurgitate to me in class, the best he could remember. I would urge him to remember as well as he could so that I could hear the rhyme for myself. He had also heard Tupac rapping a couple of times down in the basement by the cafeteria. He said he hadn't heard a great deal, but what he did hear sounded pretty good.

As time passed, other reports of the new kid's rapping prowess began to circulate through the school. One student in particular, Herb, quickly became a bona fide fan, heralding the praises of his hero without shame or exhaustion. I began to find all of this talk a bit annoying. When I next took note of the new curiosity, he was walking through the halls in blue jeans plastered with the title MC NEW YORK outlined in thick black ink, filled in red. There were various other doodles on the pants that were more a haphazard work in progress than some finished masterpiece. With the jeans, he wore a cheap-looking, nondescript button-down long-sleeve shirt and a pair of badly worn tennis shoes. His hair was cut into a two-level high-top fade, with the small section along the left side a centimeter shorter than the rest, exaggerating a part on that side. He was talking with some other new kids, primarily white faces that I did not recognize; I figured they were classmates, most likely theater students like himself. I could hear him speaking in a New York accent that, looking back, was probably more pronounced than it had to be. Still I paid the new figure on the scene no mind. He was green and brand new to what we had been developing for some time. As far as I could tell, he was like any other new kid: reserved, unsure, and relatively quiet. Again, I didn't see before me the same kid that Gerard had been telling me about, or the kid about whom Herb had been so enthusiastic.

But this would soon change. Though he began the year timid and uneasy within the new environment of the school, as awkward and clumsily dressed as the impoverished upstart adolescent he was, the new sophomore began to come into his own, outshining defiantly from within what was often laughably crude and uncoordinated without. In a natural way he began to let go of the restraints upon his hungry persona and fell comfortably into his default cockiness, boasting a definite swagger behind those unthinkable clothes, causing one to look beyond them, barely noticing.

He made friends readily, largely in the drama department, at first among the younger students with whom he shared most of his classes. I would see him between classes and around the school with these kids and think nothing of him. But it was not long before he began to find his way into the older, elite crowd which boasted the most popular, well-established students in the school: the "high-bred" brothers and sisters of DuBois's "Talented Tenth," and their white counterparts: kids with private school backgrounds, from two-parent households in the more exclusive neighborhoods in and around the city. Many of these students were fellow theater majors, their natural personality slant toward histrionics propelling them to the fore of the social scene, more so than the students of any of the other artistic disciplines. But regardless, Tupac just seemed to float into and fit into their vibe effortlessly. In no time at all he was a party to the bizarre hug fest I had witnessed with sheer awe on my first day at the strange school. "Why is everybody so happy!?" I had thought to myself that uncomfortable day, genuinely confused. It seemed as though everyone were cousins or something. I had come from a typical Baltimore City middle school where wariness hung in the air and a tough persona was of strategic importance. What I saw on my first day at the Baltimore School for the Arts, I had never seen before. But this new kid seemed to have quickly made himself at home. He appeared to be both comfortable and familiar.

From humorous and clever small talk with a definitely unfamiliar bent in and about his theater workshops and classes, to far-reaching lunchroom conversation over a bummed cigarette (made more intimate for the gesture and sacrifice), this charismatic new kid was making some very interesting friendships and gaining access to the very top of the social strata: the kind of friendships one makes sharing smoke breaks with teachers in the cafeteria, as was still common at that time, friendships that neither I nor the other rap enthusiasts had made in two or more years at the school. This was not necessarily because we couldn't; they simply represented another crew, another crowd of another ilk, from another world. Yet this skinny, poorly dressed new kid was sauntering across some invisible bridge as if there were no gorge at all. And unsatisfied with his speedy ascent among the popular kids of the school, he soon turned his attention toward our corner of the small encapsulated universe that was the School for the Arts.

Only a month or so into the year came the challenge. Apparently the upstart was really feeling himself and wished to waste no time in laying claim to his rightful place within the rap hierarchy. In fact, he went straight to the top, brazenly throwing down the gauntlet before Zorian himself. The cocky little sophomore did not plan to fit into the hierarchy; he was going to walk all over it. Of course this rocked the boat considerably. The day after the haughty challenge, Kendrick and I met up with Zorian and Ernest in the lunchroom. Tupac had heard Zorian outside and approached him. Zorian played it down, but the way Ernest told it, it was a cavalier attack upon all who represented the established rap talent in the school, a slap in the face.

Tupac and Zorian set the date for the night of the Beaux Arts Ball. I was already focused on a big performance that Gerard and I would be giving that same night in which we would become Run-DMC for an evening. It was a big deal as the ball had never before included a performance of any kind, and some teachers and administrators were against the idea. However, after working our butts off and petitioning various school personnel, we were given the okay. So my attention was focused on the approaching performance. But Ernest was persistent with his alliance-building pitch, and I agreed to say at least one rap in support of the crew at the battle.

Later that day, as Gerard and I were up on the sixth floor where the music classrooms were located, practicing for the performance, Herb walked into the room and started talking about the battle. "Pac gonna beat y'all . . . Pac gonna beat y'all," he repeated a few times. "*Y'all?* Fuck you talkin' about?" I immediately replied. The whole battle thing was their beef, Tupac and Zorian and Ernest. I had agreed to lend some support, but I wasn't thinking about that. "Y'all gonna be rappin'?" he asked. "Yeah, we gonna be rappin'," I replied, but I was talking as much about the performance as anything. That's what I was hyped about. We had always seen our friends and others in the dance and music departments performing and shining before the school, on stage. As visual artists, painters and sculptors and such, we never had the chance to perform. This was Gerard's and my big opportunity to shine, to make a name for ourselves in the school.

"Man, I'm telling you, man, he gonna beat *all* y'all," Herb persisted with an annoying smile.

"Man, whatever, man. Fuck you. Who the fuck is *Pac*? Fuck Pac. Shit, *this* is gonna be the shit. This *Run-DMC* shit!" I had heard enough about this dude. I hate to hear people all up on somebody's nuts, like Herb was all up on Tupac's. Especially when I feel I'm good myself. Gerard and I blew Herb off and went back to what we were doing.

The following afternoon out in front of the school, I was caught off guard when I noticed the stringy new character walking directly toward me from the front doorway. I was talking with Kendrick. We were winding down from the school day, standing at the bottom of the steps by the railing. Without a hint of hesitation and full of arrogance, the new guy easily approached Kendrick and me with a particularly matter-of-fact expression on his face, stopping at the top step and looking down on us as if he had scripted it that way. He looked me dead in the eyes. "So y'all gonna be in the battle?" he asked in a voice that smacked of mockery. Immediately, I knew that Herb had given a report, most likely an inflated report, on our conversation from the day before. We hesitated for a split second, taken aback by his directness, but answered with a resounding "Yeah!", eyebrows furrowed and chests pumped out.

His challenge was too public and too void of deference for us to even consider backing out. And I harbored no such thought until some time later when the big performance and all of its requisite parts and preparation returned to my realm of consciousness. The battle was Zorian's beef; somehow, I had become involved. But still, my sights were set on the unprecedented performance. The next two weeks were spent practicing and preparing for it. The impending battle barely crossed my mind.

As our musical support, Gerard and I enlisted Todd Miller, who was the best guitar player in the school, and John Tamokis, who was the best drummer. With great attention to detail, the four of us worked the two-song routine to an exact science. We were performing "Perfection," and "Walk This Way" by Run-DMC. This was our big opportunity. When the day arrived, we were ready.

The ball began at eight o'clock in the evening. The school took on a different look, a different vibe in the evening. There were new shadows, new things highlighted under the concentrated glare of unusually bright lights; a haunting silence periodically broken by random sound. The dark, skinny halls stacked upon each other seven stories high in the retrofitted antique hotel were like mysterious catacombs, resonating with the faint-sounding music of late-night dance exercises from some far-off corner of the school, or the echo of two lone voices reciting lines.

Gerard and I emerged from the locker room on the basement floor decked in our Run-DMC outfits of black imitation leather

pants and jackets, Shell Head Adidas with no shoestrings, black
T-shirts, fake fat gold chains, and black hats. Completing the effect,
I donned a pair of fake Gazelle eyeglasses, black with gold color
around the lenses. With an air of expectation, we climbed the basement steps to the first floor and entered the ballroom. It was already teeming with people dressed in all sorts of strange outfits,
from guys in long dresses and heavy makeup to the more traditional
costumes of Dracula and the like. Two years before I might have
found this spectacle shocking and unnerving, but as a veteran of the
school I was duly desensitized; it was normal. All I now saw around
me was a growing audience. After half an hour or so of milling
around and enjoying the party, the four of us walked up on stage
and got ready. Seeing us take the stage, everyone redirected their
attention. Before I knew it Todd and John were rockin' it like professional musicians on the drums and electric guitar; Gerard and I
easily got into the flow. Swaggering comfortably about the stage we
hit every line perfectly, like clockwork. We sounded good. I felt like
a star up there, working the enthusiastic crowd, doing all of Run-
DMC's signature moves and mannerisms perfectly and having a
ball. It was even better than I had hoped.

Toward the end of our first song, "Perfection," I spotted Tupac
in the crowd. There was no hint of admiration in his eyes. He stood
there, still, oblivious to the hyped-up students around him. A
shorter, equally thin, brown-skinned guy was standing next to him,
also still. They appeared to be together. When my eyes met Tupac's
he locked on, glaring at me squarely, challenging, and voicing with
his very eyes, "You ready?" He held no regard for my moment in
the sun. I tried not to look at him again; my little taste of pubescent
fame, my long-awaited, carefully planned moment in the spotlight
he wished nothing more than to take from me. But I couldn't help

it and glanced back several times; and still the same stolid expression, no detection of any movement in either of them. I brushed it off through the remainder of the short set, but it remained in the back of my mind.

When we finished, Gerard and I raised our fists in the air victoriously, smiling widely to the cheers of the crowd, many of whom probably didn't know our names despite the smallness of the school and its student body. I stepped down from the stage eager to collect the praise of my friends and curious looks of interest from those I didn't know; but Tupac would have none of it. As my forward foot hit the ballroom floor after stepping down from the stage, the skinny kid dressed as if for a school dance of an entirely different sort, black dress shoes, black slacks of polyester or some similar-looking material, a dark cardigan sweater and dark dress shirt underneath (almost the same exact outfit I had seen him in several times before in school), walked right up to me. "You ready?" he said coldly, exactly as I had heard it the first time while in the midst of the performance. There was nothing to do but reply in the affirmative and abort my hard-earned victory lap, setting out instead to collect Zorian and the rest of the crew.

In the middle of the crowded ballroom Tupac immediately entered a zone, what I would later come to recognize as *his* zone. A switch tripped inside him. "Come on y'all. We gonna battle. . . . We gonna battle," he said several times, corralling the students around him, motioning toward the door of the ballroom. Now the spotlight would rest where it should, where it belonged as far as he was concerned—on him.

We walked out of the ballroom into the hall, and down the steps leading to the lunchroom and locker rooms, the crowd growing with every step. I looked down to my shoestringless Adidas flopping about and slapping against the tile: Gerard and I were still clad in our slick black outfits. Zorian, Kendrick, and Ernest were in regular clothes. I fidgeted with my glasses. The gold coloring of the frame gleamed under the fluorescent light of the lamps. The whole way down the steps I fingered the iconic representation of the very soul of the hip-hop culture, as if to summon some hidden genie more so than to achieve a more comfortable alignment.

When we hit the basement floor we all stopped in the hall outside the cafeteria, near the locker rooms. The crowd gathered around us, Tupac and the friend of his who none of us had seen before, Zorian, Kendrick, Ernest, and me. Gerard, deferring to the four of us in regard to rhyming talent, stood off to the side, making himself one of the crowd. Tupac posted up against the wall, leaning against it with his arms folded, looking completely unconcerned and at ease. He introduced his companion as Mouse (aka Dana), a partner of his from his neighborhood. After everyone settled around in a circle it was immediately obvious why Mouse was there. "Yo D, box!" Tupac exclaimed, just as LL Cool J had in that tense scene in *Krush Groove*. Mouse's beatbox ripped through the crowd of students influencing all to begin moving in time. Broad smiles erupted on bobbing heads. Several softly voiced expletives expressing approval peppered the air. . . . It was on.

Right on beat Tupac stood himself up and jumped in with a dope-ass rhyme. "You can't stop me!" he hurled from deep inside, kicking off the battle with authority, rockin' it! The two of them were in perfect harmony, playing off one another, bouncing lyrics back and forth like a perfectly passed ball maneuvered too quickly for the eye to follow. It was clear they had practiced extensively. From the very first moment it was painfully obvious that we had entered an arena in which we did not belong, one in which we were obviously underexperienced and unfamiliar. The two-man hit squad of cardigan sweater–donning sophomores who looked more like altar boys than rap artists crushed the four of us decisively. With unbelievable skill and precision execution they nailed each and every line of each rhyme.

After Zorian and the rest of our crew ran out of rhymes they continued on, ripping more than seven in total before it was all over. Zorian, Ernest, and Kendrick were quickly demoralized, surrendering early on. I saw Gerard join in with the crowd, jockin' all of Tupac and Mouse's stuff, but I refused to concede defeat so easily. Desperately, I relaunched an attack, resorting to old, stale rhymes since I had exhausted all of my current material. But it was useless. After my last relatively sad attempt, they dropped the sickle on our necks, delivering the final blow. As if in reply to what I had just thrown out in desperation, they busted out with, "You're Talkin' That Bullshit!", their grand finale. Everyone completely zapped out at this. Mouse went crazy on the beatbox and the entire crowd danced along, yelling out their approval, jeering. In grand fashion Tupac had dethroned Zorian and won the distinction of undisputed King of Rap. And we were embarrassed in front of what seemed to be the entire student body. I cannot explain to you the full extent of the embarrassment. Not only was I denied the fruits of my well-orchestrated moment in the limelight, but I was humiliated in its stead. That night I saw exactly what had gotten Herb so hyped. This kid was extremely talented.

 **Roland Park**

Tupac's tenure in Baltimore began in the winter of 1984 when he arrived from New York with his sister and mother at age thirteen. His first day of school proved to be typical of his life and suggestive of the recurring tragedy that would haunt him until the final curtain. The zone school for his neighborhood was Roland Park Middle. Although a magnet school as well, attracting many of the brightest students from around the Baltimore area, and one of the top two public middle schools in the city, Roland Park Middle had in its zone some of the worst neighborhoods in the metropolitan area. Located in the northeast section of Baltimore, the school served several of the poorest communities and most notorious drug hot spots: namely Tupac's own neighborhood, the Greenmount Avenue–Old York Road corridor. Consequently, the school could be a difficult environment.

On his first day in mid-November he walked into homeroom late, conspicuous under the spotlight shone over the heads of the class long since seated. He wore baggy pants of thin blue fabric, like surgical scrubs, with staples encircling the bottom of each leg along the hem. The pants hung loosely from his skinny frame, below a generic long-sleeve shirt tucked in at the waist where a drawstring held the rag-tag ensemble in place. His hair was lopsided, like some two-tiered wannabe Bobby Brown cut. And he exposed poorly kept, unfinished braces along both rows of teeth with every parting of his lips. Only the metal anchors were in place on each tooth; no wires connected them. Not only did he enter this potentially brutal environment looking like a walking target, but he did so almost three months into the school year, after all of the students had long since felt each other out and made their key alliances for the year.

Employing little fanfare, Ms. Gee, the teacher, acknowledged the new student's presence and pointed him to an open seat. Within seconds of his taking it, an unusually large boy returned from the bathroom and marched straight up to him. Apparently the teacher had unwittingly led the new student to an occupied seat. Sensing the opportunity for an incident, students began to egg on Fat Will with taunts of "Bang'nat nigga!" and "Take your shit back" when the oversized, two-time eighth grader demanded, in front of the class, that Tupac get up. But the funny-looking, skinny new kid would not be swayed, and stood up to the much larger challenger defiantly, in his face.

"Ms. Gee told me to sit here," Tupac told Fat Will, refusing to move. "She don't see no problem with it," he argued indignantly before Ms. Gee quickly stepped in to break up the fray, apologizing from her desk for the oversight and asking Tupac to take another seat. He had only followed instructions. Yet he found himself faced with a certain beat-down in front of his new classmates, all because of his steadfast refusal to acquiesce behind someone else's error.

The kids of the school, and his neighborhood for that matter, did not take to Tupac very well at all. To them he looked funny, like some kind of square reject type. At that time in Baltimore, clothing was the key. Baltimore sistas looked first to a guy's tennis shoes for their initial, most lasting impression. And by the time their eyes reached his face, they had taken in his entire ensemble from socks to hat. Within Baltimore's variety of the growing hip-hop culture there was a strict dress code. For every type of clothing there were several brands from which to choose and no deviation was permitted. There were certain brands of jeans, tennis shoes, sweat suits, jackets, shorts, and even undershirts and glasses; the expensive undershirts were worn as shirts, and the gaudy, heavy gold-rimmed glasses bore no suggestion of intellectualism. The boys defiantly thought of themselves as Slick-Heads, or Yo-Boys. And these Slick-Heads distinguished themselves primarily through the brands and abundance of their clothing. Underlying the outer display was the insinuation of thuggery with regard to one's ability to acquire and retain such expensive and showy articles in the midst of poverty and want. Drug dealing and robbery were already common ingredients in and around the lives of the young middle-schoolers. During this period, young boys were regularly sticking each other up and even murdering one another for lambskin coats, Starter NBA/college jackets, patent leather tennis shoes, gold chains, and even gold teeth. It was all about attitude/heart. And in Baltimore City, attitude and attire were one.

Although Tupac had plenty of attitude, always carrying about him a certain defiant flavor, for this fiercely strict dress code he possessed none of the expected items. Nor did he have an imposing physique or demeanor with which to trump the process. As Mouse later put it, "He tried to have a B-Boy thang goin' on, but the brokeness always showed through." Tupac's mother was far too poor to buy him any of the expensive items, and probably too sophisticated to fall prey to such nonsense if she could. And Tupac was much more artist than hustler or stick-up bandit, so he went without. And so he was dismissed out of hand.

However, for Tupac, this painful rebuke and contempt from his peers only meant valuable space in which to realize, years ahead of his time, his own interests and deepest passions. Unencumbered with the flustering barrage of perceived limit and "normal" daily thought typical to the, in some real sense, distracted development of a mainstream socialite, Tupac explored the depths of his desire and potential in rap and drama with unbelievable focus and intensity. His maturity in general, as well as the maturity of his work in these areas, was exceptional.

On his third day at the school, the students were instructed to recite in music class their original poems which they had completed for homework the previous night. No one took the effort seriously, laughing clumsily through their lame, half-hearted attempts. Many offered the half-plagiarized, inflated words of Hallmark cards and the like, but Tupac's piece was entirely different. He presented an impressive poem that intelligently detailed his love for a girl. It was a masterful consideration of the finer nuance in the relationship between love and beauty, true beauty, and how the latter had set ablaze the former. So well thought out and skillfully presented was this unmatched piece that not even the most ignorant and defiant attempted to satirize or ridicule.

When, later that day, he boarded the bus to go home, he found all of the seats taken except for one next to a short guy from his class who had been the principal instigator two days before during the incident with Fat Will. Only after Tupac walked all the way up to the guy and asked loudly, "Excuse me," did the guy begrudgingly move his book bag from the seat and allow Tupac to sit down. The tension was thick. Neither of them said anything to each other for quite some time, Tupac sitting quietly and the guy steadily engaging all of those around him in conversation. Finally, the guy turned to Tupac and broke the ice by telling him that he liked his poem from earlier that day. "I liked yours too," Tupac replied, accepting the gesture. The guy then asked Tupac where he lived and where he was from. Tupac replied that he was from New York but he was currently living on Greenmount Avenue. It turned out that they lived in the very same East Baltimore neighborhood, their homes only blocks apart. The guy's name was Mouse. Tupac kicked another rhyme that Mouse really liked. And Mouse invited him to the neighborhood playground to hang out. Mouse would later realize that the rhyme Tupac kicked on the bus that day as his own was really a Kurtis Blow cut not yet familiar in Baltimore. Tupac was well aware of the advantage afforded him by the pioneering spirit of his hometown. And he would use his New York experience, his New York identity, repeatedly throughout his development as an artist and as a young man.

Widely known around the neighborhood, Mouse was king of the beatbox and little nephew to the sultans of the neighborhood dope trade. This status he also enjoyed in school as everyone in the neighborhood attended the same one, Roland Park. At school, in the valuable minutes between classes, the boys would regularly congregate in the halls or bathrooms where a cipher would easily take shape. The big thing of the day was break dancing, and this was always the focus, each of the boys showing off his latest moves. Lyricism and rhyming hadn't yet taken hold in Baltimore. The music was primarily imported from New York and Philadelphia, while the broader tenets of hip-hop, especially break dancing, were a way of life, to be mastered and flaunted.

Mouse would often call these ciphers to order, sending an irresistibly loud and infectious beatbox careening through the halls, amplified masterfully by the adept positioning of the source with respect to the surrounding walls, floor, and ceiling. In the hallway guys might begin to chant, in unison, the latest jam out on the radio, or join in on the beat with the help of surrounding lockers. And in the bathrooms they would quickly break down to the floor and bust out their latest move, whether it be a windmill with no hands, flailing feet barely missing the sinks along the wall and quickly reacting onlookers, or a head spin, done in a wool skullcap worn to school specifically for the purpose.

As classmates, and in such close proximity to each other in the neighborhood, Tupac and Mouse quickly gelled together. Within a matter of days they were hanging together as much in school as in the neighborhood. As Mouse's friend, and a genuine hip-hop enthusiast in his own right, Tupac naturally gravitated to the hallway/bathroom sessions despite all of the cracks and overt resistance to his acceptance. He was certainly no break-dancer, or a dancer of any kind for that matter. But, as was the case with most young black kids in the inner cities of America in the eighties, he and hip-hop were one. And wherever the growing culture was taking root and sprouting most gloriously, he could be found making offerings of water and his own special nourishment.

Tupac's thing was flow. Rhyme skills. Coming from New York,

where the making of the music was as big a pursuit for cats on the street as was vibing around it and dancing to it, and being clumsily unsuited for the latter, Tupac's focus was different from that of the kids in Baltimore at the time. When cats did take the hip-hop vibe beyond the arena of dance and into a more lyrical appreciation of the delicious beats employed to fuel the ciphers (i.e., beatbox, banging on books and walls, floor stomping, etc.), reciting lyrics to their favorite songs, Tupac had a habit of jumping in with his own material wherever a lull would permit. Enthusiastically he would kick off a rhyme as if in one of these same ciphers in New York, dropping verses like he was on stage. But his offerings were always met with the same indignant and unpleasant looks from everyone around, who would almost cringe at the sound of the unfamiliar lyrics. He hadn't the clothes, and he hadn't the dancing ability. And they saw nothing to be appreciated. They often asked Mouse why he hung out with the strange-looking "reject." But Mouse was drawn to Tupac's energy, to his heart, and to his exceptional rapping ability. Their close friendship quickly evolved and revolved around rap. It was the burning passion attracting them to one another and equally consuming them both. Every day they got together, either at the rec center or playground, both literally right outside Tupac's back door, or at either of their homes, if not all of the above in succession. At Tupac's they would craft rhymes in his poorly lit room at the very back of his mother's apartment (actually a makeshift partition to the downtrodden row house sticking out, conspicuously, from its parent structure in the rear). And at Mouse's they would be down in the basement, writing and rehearsing rhymes while Mouse's grandfather worked on some project or the other in his little shop area in the back, listening to James Brown, Sam Cook, or one of his other favorites. Or they would be down there blasting music on Mouse's little tape player, connected directly to one huge trebleless speaker donated to the cause by his grandfather who, as a trucker, always had innumerable odds and ends from his travels crammed into the shop space.

Without hesitation the boys went about the business of composing songs, needing no buffer period of acquaintance. Before two weeks had passed on their new friendship, their first rhyme was complete: clearly written out on notebook paper in sections to denote verses and chorus. It was not much longer before the challenge of successfully completing a song evolved into one of doing so in a single day, and then less, and then a matter of minutes. Everything was a competition among the kids of the neighborhood. When they were running it was, "Who was the fastest?" When they were pitching nickels it was, "Who was winnin' the most money?" When playing basketball it was, "Who could ball the best?" And it became the same for writing rhymes: "Who could write the most?" They would actually use the clock to race, seeing who could write the most in a given span of time.

"Naw, yo ... Y'handwritin's bigger," Mouse mimics a typical scene from so many years before, holding out an invisible sheet of paper as if comparing it to another next to it. People would later take note of Tupac's extraordinary ability to walk into a studio and write out a new song in no time at all.

Religiously, they practiced every day, almost obsessively. Their favorite practice environment was inside a large plastic bubble off to the side of the playground. With three openings in the sides for ground access and one at its crest in the middle with a metal pole through the top for children to slide down, the bubble provided perfect acoustics for the purpose of loud rhyming and mimicking the popular echo effect found in many of the recordings of that period. However this bubble was not theirs alone and doubled as a rest room for the different hustlers who would set up shop in and around the playground. As such, it reeked of urine. But still this did not keep at bay the enthusiastic upstarts. With numerous little barrel-shaped Hug juices purchased for free with the food stamps of dope fiends who wanted only the converted change in return, the starry-eyed young boys would douse the ground inside, all along the circumference of the structure, to make more manageable the environmental conditions, and then proceed through the full reper- toire of their songs as if in a comfortable studio.

On occasion police cars would pull into the alleys leading into the playground, sealing the major exits. The officers would then fan out for a random sweep of everyone on the premises. Their favorite target area was the fenced-in basketball court from which there was no escape. In one such instance Tupac found himself caught inside this fenced-in area, and was searched along with everyone else in- side, even forced to take off his shoes. This was routine. The offi- cers would check everyone in a random fishing expedition, hoping to catch hustlers who hadn't thought quickly enough, or the prod- uct of those who had craftily gotten it into the care of a younger kid, safely below the low-hanging noose of the legal system.

Such an experience was common for the boys. It was common for everyone in the neighborhood, for everyone in all similar neighborhoods throughout the country. But from this seedier side of the goings-on in the neighborhood, Mouse was largely shielded and protected. The watchful eye of his vigilant uncle, the younger of the two, closest to him in age, followed every movement outside of the home with intense scrutiny. At home Mouse's grandparents and legal guardians, probably the most strict and religious older cou- ple in the area, were the cornerstone to this family buffer, creating for him a world, inside that of the depressed East Baltimore neighborhood, filled with lessons and accountability. Only if he had gone to church could he ride his bike for half an hour on Sunday, the Lord's day. But having no such buffer, Tupac was out there, from time to time, freely, in the middle of it all. At one point he even asked for an opportunity to work, but was clowned by the considerably older hustlers, more for being too young (and probably for being too close to Mouse) than anything else.

Through Mouse, Tupac had gotten to know everyone around the way. Otherwise he would have certainly remained an outcast—disliked and scorned. There was just something about him, beyond even his utterly unacceptable wears, that seemed to deliver to him, without fail, negativity and aggression. And he would never do anything to provoke it. It just came to him, like the mail. Mouse remembers a certain look, of blankness, of void, eyes glazed over at the onset of some painful disappointment, some humiliation. It was exactly the same every time: a spontaneously visible callus over the self, developed from years of rubbing.

People seemed to always act and react negatively toward Tupac. I would later see the same mysterious dynamic, and the same look in response; neither Mouse nor I can explain it, but it was something very real that we witnessed *many* times throughout our travels with him.

Although Tupac would catch endless flak from many in the neighborhood until his last day there, his close association to Mouse delivered him from much of this, bringing him a fair amount of acceptance. The two of them would often rap for Mouse's uncle and all of his uncle's boys, who would always give them much dap and dollar bills offered boastfully between the competing hustlers, as much to compliment the donor as the recipient. This helped a great deal in providing Tupac relief and tolerance in the neighborhood. And financially (there were usually fives and tens mixed among the ones), it was, immediately, a well to which he and Mouse returned often. They were always performing and rehearsing, for anybody and everybody. Ms. Shakur regularly found herself the subject of serenade. The boys would offer their fresh fruits, from only the most authentic hip-hop inspiration, with seriousness and purpose. To the new cultural movement taking over the inner cities of America they were devout disciples, and offspring, organically connected. Ms. Shakur enjoyed the way the boys asserted themselves. Her support for them never wavered.

A friend of hers and of the family, Bobby, was a musician who was often around their apartment. Upon hearing the boys, Bobby took them to a couple jam sessions with his band down in his basement. Showing no fear or apprehension, the duo took hold of the mikes confidently, proceeding through their rhymes as if they had been granted studio time and should not waste it. The band followed behind them, providing energetic beats. Within their short time there the boys even composed a couple pieces: one, a largely instrumental refrain with which they would soon close out their flawless inaugural public performance, only weeks away.

3 First Shows

In the neighborhood was a man named Roger who was closely tied into the entertainment network in the city. His little nephew was something of a local celebrity, regularly performing a popular seventh inning stretch Michael Jackson routine atop the Orioles dugout. Roger, through both his brother who worked at a popular Baltimore radio station as well as his own endeavors, knew all of the promoters, club owners, and radio personalities around town, and therefore had the inside track on all of the events and contests. The first of his offerings to Tupac and Mouse came in February of 1985. He arranged a spot for them on the bill of a Mantronix show, also featuring Just Ice, at the Cherry Hill Recreation Center. Increasingly excited about their approaching debut, the boys began to practice over at Roger's house, where they hooked up with a neighborhood DJ to provide music for the repertoire of songs that didn't have any up to that point. Although their songs were generally lyrical collaborations, supporting music was a luxury, and Mouse's exceptional beatbox an asset that could not be wasted. Consequently, Mouse would simply curtail or forgo his verses altogether, his beatbox being central, the glue binding it all together. But he didn't mind this a great deal. Beatboxing was something he genuinely loved. However, for the special occasion of the upcoming show, they would bring along a DJ. The young crew also needed a name. Expending little time or energy on the task they decided on the direct and to the point "Eastside Crew."

The evening of their first public performance began on a treacherously snowy winter day fraught with confrontation and confusion. Watching snow accumulate on the ground from his bedroom, Mouse innocently donned new snowsuit pants of his uncle's, preparing to head over to Tupac's and then to Roger's to rehearse. He suited up liberally, making himself resistant to the cold and swirling wind. Along with the bottom half of the snowsuit he wore sweat pants, a T-shirt and sweater, his own winter jacket, and a wool skullcap. Protected and numb, he walked out the door to Tupac's, where he found his partner waiting anxiously. The two of them walked over to Roger's. The DJ, Buddha, was there with his new turntable in hand.

After hours of rehearsing and chilling over at Roger's, where there was a pseudo home studio—Casio keyboard and Sp1100, drum set—there was a knock at the door. When Roger opened it, there stood Mouse's uncle, noticeably drunk and particularly perturbed about something.

"Gimme my fuckin' snow pants!" he gruffly barked as Mouse approached the front door.

"What?!" Mouse replied, stunned.

"Gimme my mawfuckin' snow pants!"

"I was gonna wear'm tonight. We gotta show . . . I was gonna ask you but you weren't home an' . . ."

"Gimme my mawfuckin' snow pants! Take'm off now!"

The two of them walked outside with Mouse trying to defuse the situation and calm his irrational uncle. While pleading to be allowed to walk home (only a block away) in order to take off and hand over his uncle's property, and refusing, flatly, to disrobe on the spot as he was so vehemently instructed, he noticed in his periphery a dark blur quickly approaching his face from the left. Having the edge on his drunk uncle with regard to reflexes, he was able to duck the fist that probably would have knocked him out cold. By this time Tupac and Buddha had come out of the house and quickly ran over to help. Buddha, who was a little older than Tupac and Mouse, was able to get behind the drunk uncle and pull his jacket up over his head, disabling him. When they let go, Tupac and Buddha darted back inside and Mouse ran home with his uncle following behind, having a hard time with the snow. Unable to catch his little nephew before reaching the refuge of home and grandparents, the irate uncle gave up the chase.

Angry and disoriented, wearing a pair of his own jeans, Mouse met back up with the group over at Roger's house. Big John, one of the more imposing young brothers in the neighborhood, had joined them; he wouldn't be performing but his presence was very much welcome considering where they were headed. At around ten o'clock the four boys and Roger piled into Roger's car and set out on the slippery, snow-filled journey down to Cherry Hill. More ominous than the ride itself was the destination. No one in the car was happy to be headed for Cherry Hill, particularly on such a treacherous and unpredictable night. Tupac hadn't been in Baltimore long enough to understand the notorious reputation of the part of town to which they were headed, but the fact that these veterans were visibly uneasy made him quite nervous.

When they arrived at the building, Roger steered the car around to the back where they parked. He knew exactly where to go, leading them to a door along the side that was partially open. The door led backstage, where Roger ran into various acquaintances including his brother and Chuck Mack, the MC of the evening with whom his brother worked at the radio station, and the promoter of the event. Hearing the music blaring, the irresistible beat reverberating through their small frames, the boys headed straight to the side of the stage where they saw Mantronix under a spotlight, working feverishly with the crowded mixing setup laid out in front of him.

"Yo, Mantronix white!" one of them acknowledged as the group gathered at the side of the stage. The next realization was that they were in what appeared to be more a glorified high school gymnasium than concert hall. Beyond the stage was completely black, and they could see very little from where they were standing. Yet despite the sea of blackness before them it was obvious the place was packed.

"Yo, who this white boy?!" they all continued to ask rhetorically, not yet ready to accept what they saw; but all doubt was dismissed straightaway. The tall, somewhat goofy looking "white boy" (actually he was Puerto Rican) was rockin' it! *Sweatin'!* behind that table over some kind of huge, opened-up suitcase full of strange music machinery and mixing equipment. The whole vibe was unreal.

Mantronix was out there kicking stuff they had never heard before. At one point he just stopped the record and bounced it on the turntable for a minute, making it feel like an earthquake inside the building. That night they saw a whole new level of DJing, a whole new level of hip-hop. Buddha strained his neck the entire time, investigating the equipment to see if there were some special kind of turntables.

Next was Just Ice and DMX* (Just Ice's beatbox). Mouse watched intently as the well-known duo from New York took the stage. He was a true Just Ice fan, their hit single "I'm Leaving" being one of his favorite songs. With the introduction to their first song and subsequent first few bars, everything, immediately, turned even stranger than it had been to that point. The sound of DMX's crisp and familiar beatbox caused Mouse to consider for the first time the simmering fear within that had been giving off noxious fumes the entire day, increasingly so since their arrival backstage. The young beatbox/lyricist had walked the gauntlet that day through heavy snowfall and blows thrown by the man whom he respected more than any other, and all under the looming uncertainty of this huge show. Yet present and growing within the uncomfortable mist of the strange evening was acknowledgment of the fact that "I can *take* this mawfucka!" Mouse thought to himself while looking on from the side of the stage. The well-nurtured and developed instinct to battle kicked in.

After Just Ice and DMX rocked their set, it was Tupac and Mouse's turn. The arrangers of the evening must have squeezed the boys in at the last minute. MC T, who was headlining with Mantronix, had not yet taken the stage, but certainly the young duo was not supposed

---

*not to be confused with the DMX of current fame (note aka Earl Simmons)

to follow such a prominent group. When they were announced to
the crowd as the Eastside Crew, the shortcoming of their name was
embarrassingly obvious.

"I mean, we really didn't get any boos or nuthin'," Mouse recalls
about the reaction from the Cherry Hill crowd. But the atmosphere
was less than enthusiastic. However, the two-man crew brushed this
aside. Beyond the first two rows of people it was completely dark,
making the crowd something of an unseen non-factor to them. It
was time to perform, and they did what they knew. . . . It was on.

They started off with "Nigga Please," a rhyme about the exploits
and tactics of a young, wannabe lady's man. To this humorous song
Mouse provided a slow and deliberate drum and snare beat, at the
breaks of which he would come to an abrupt stop, chiming in
loudly with the title refrain (as if from one of the uninterested
women in reply to Tupac's overtures): *"Nigga please!"* This loosened
up the crowd considerably, getting them going a little. But it was
deeper into their five-song medley set when Mouse broke into an
all-out organic "beat fest" that the crowd really got going. The
boys played off of this energy, which they rode through the rest of
the performance. For their final song, Buddha appeared on stage
carrying a record that he handed to Mantronix, who then placed it
on the turntable. His big DJing debut consisted of standing out on
stage next to Mantronix, holding an empty record cover. The song
was "Rock On," the largely instrumental piece Tupac and Mouse
had composed at Bobby's house along with his band. To take the
place of the band they had found among the many records in Buddha's crates an old instrumental that fit perfectly. The two-man
crew closed out the show together, each rapping a verse and at the
end repeating the hypnotic refrain: "Rock on! . . . Rock on!"

Enthusiastically, they walked off stage. They hadn't filled the arena with wild applause at their exit. But they knew they had ripped. The crowd had reacted favorably, swaying with the music, the sound system was excellent, and there were no mistakes. After accepting the kind words of many backstage, they resumed their place at the side of the stage to watch MC T and Mantronix. Roger offered them only one major critique on their performance. Apparently the stage was both long and deep, providing for a great deal of space. And the boys never left each other at its middle through the entire performance.

"We was used to: 'Right here!' You know what I'm sayin'?" Mouse explains, laughing, hunched over and holding an imaginary mike as if kickin' a rhyme in the middle of a small cipher of peers. "Me and you, baby . . . come'oin, an' less do this!" he adds, gesturing to an invisible person beside him, also hunched over in place, bobbing to a beat, kickin' rhymes.

After the show Roger and his brother got to talking backstage. His brother was interested in the two neighborhood boys. They called Tupac and Mouse over. At their request Tupac kicked a verse. The boys then transitioned into another beatbox display with Tupac leading the flow, interjecting adeptly: "And uh! . . . With uh! . . . Kick it! . . ." as Mouse followed seamlessly behind, each time changing the beat to something even more nasty than the last. They held back and saved nothing, effecting looks of amazed delight in the eyes of the two men watching them. DMX had been nearby and heard the whole thing. He was so impressed by the display that he felt obligated to join in and attempt to out do them, but he couldn't come close. Several times he jumped in and put forth his best, only to be crushed by Mouse's reply. The thirteen-year-old boys, only several months acquainted, had battled down proven stars.

In the weeks following the show, Tupac and Mouse were contacted by a representative of Jive Records. Virgil Simms, manager of Mantronix and responsible for the emergence of EPMD, as well as other prominent hip-hop artists, had been in the crowd and had contacted Roger's brother at the radio station. Roger then announced the exciting news to Tupac and Mouse. Apparently Mr. Simms was very impressed with the youngsters and was considering the possibility of signing them. Roger drove the boys out to the radio station to meet the industry mover and shaker, at which time Mr. Simms formally presented his desire to sign them. It was all quite fantastical for the boys, who drove back to the neighborhood triumphant and abuzz with anticipation; but it was not to be. Ms. Shakur would have nothing of it, and flatly refused to allow Tupac to pursue the relationship. She felt that the thirteen-year-olds had more important things to think about at that time in their lives, that they had a lot more growing up to do before entering into a commitment so all-encompassing and so intertwined with the very sorts of people and power against which she had struggled as a Black Panther her entire adult life.

The sting of this sobering decision burned in them for a period, but soon waned and passed, as do most things at that age. They continued in the same manner as they had since meeting, with even greater confidence and drive than before, now with tangible proof of the unique value of their skill. Tupac would invoke Virgil Simms's name many times in the years to come, as if he and Mouse had a firm contact and record deal ever waiting for them in the wings of their combined life, needing only to be claimed.

Day in and day out they practiced, always ready, and finely tuned. And now they were officially a group, with name and résumé. Happily, they took on and destroyed all comers, while returning often to their bread-and-butter performances in the neighborhood for the hustlers on the corners from whom they could always count on spending cash.

Their next formal performance came later that summer in the form of a citywide talent contest commemorating the fiftieth birthday of the Enoch Pratt Free Library. Tupac had found out about the competition and submitted a written entry consisting of lyrics to a new rap about the important role of the library in the community, and about the importance of reading in general. Somehow Tupac had a knack for finding out about all sorts of competitions around town. Roger would come to them with tips every so often, but Tupac always had some performance or contest brewing, if not several at a time. And they could be in the most obscure places, sponsored by the most obscure organizations. To this day, neither I nor Mouse has any good idea of how he was able to do this; somehow he always knew of them. It seemed to Mouse that every time he turned around, Tupac would not just inform him of some new contest, but that they had already been entered and would be performing on such and such a date.

The written submission for the Enoch Pratt contest made the cut and the two-man group was invited to the semifinals at the branch of the library on the corner of Pennsylvania and North Avenues in West Baltimore. When they arrived at the location on the day of the contest, there was a good-size crowd already assembled. People were seated in chairs arranged in a semicircle about six rows deep around an open floor space where the performances were given. Like a well-crafted, well-oiled machine, the boys burst into their performance with surprising poise and exactness, distinguishing themselves from the rest of the field. Easily, they emerged from this second round of competition (the first being the written submissions) as finalists, making quite an impression on the organizer of the event, Ms. Taylor. When they informed Ms. Taylor of their troubles finding a ride and that it would probably be no different the next time, she didn't hesitate to offer her assistance for the final, which would be held at the main branch of the library on Cathedral Street downtown. On the day of the event, Ms. Taylor remained true to her word and showed up on time at Tupac's mother's apartment on Greenmount Avenue, where the boys were waiting. The performances were given in a huge room to the rear of the impressive building only blocks away from the business district of the city and Inner Harbor. As Ms. Taylor later remembered, Tupac and Mouse's performance stood out from the rest at this final round of competition as well. In this, their first formal competition, a citywide affair, they were awarded first place. This immediately became the standard for them and they would expect or accept no less.

While the two young boys, now fourteen years old, practiced their rhymes every day without fail, they were still children, and not at all of the scholarly, homework-intensive tradition. So they were able to find ample time for other activities. Mouse was big on basketball, and gave equal attention to football, pool, or whatever other kind of game was kicked off in the rec center or outside among the neighborhood boys. Although Tupac would join in from time to time, this was often time not shared between them, since Tupac was a bit challenged in the coordination and athleticism department. Tupac was also not particularly interested in parties, while Mouse was very much about the social scene. Tupac was often happy to just stay in the house and compose rhymes. It seemed that all Tupac wanted to do was write rhymes; he was always writing. But this probably had as much to do with what he wished to avoid on the party scene as it did with his love for writing. Parties and other social affairs were something for which Tupac was ill equipped, and he would rather skip the whole thing than force the issue, only to receive the same subtle and not so subtle bludgeoning he had come to expect from his peers. Mouse, on the other hand, had no such worries. Not that his family was well off, or even middle class for that matter. Despite his humble living arrangements (in the three-bedroom home, he and his two uncles shared a room; his sister, mother, and aunt were in another; and his grandparents occupied the third), Mouse always had all of the nicest clothes. In an attempt to keep him from being tempted by the various opportunities for fast cash, his grandmother would buy him all of the latest fashions, the same coveted things that the drug dealers sported with such pride just so long as he was "good." And being in such close quarters to his uncles, who always had cash to spend, he often received little treats from them also.

The material imbalance between the two young friends was painfully obvious. And although no blow-ups ever arose as a result of this delicate situation, there was a definite unspoken tension: How could there not be? Mouse's enviably clean appearance was in stark contrast to that of his awkwardly dressed new friend who couldn't help but take note; he had grown up noticing, and wanting. But Mouse's indifference to Tupac's unglamorous appearance was sincere. It was something the boys never discussed.

When they went to the movies and Tupac had only a dollar, Mouse would always have another to make the required fare. Along with his weekly allowance from his grandparents, Mouse also held down an after-school job cleaning up at the neighborhood day care center, for which he made thirty-six dollars a week. He quickly included his friend in the spoils of this lucrative arrangement, inviting Tupac to help him out with the daily chores, and splitting the wages down the middle. The job was a daily recreation for them. Mouse had been given keys to the place so they routinely stopped through in the evening after everyone had left for the day. Although the young boys always made sure the job was complete before leaving, they spent as much time playing around in the small deserted building. Along with vacuuming, sweeping, wiping down desks, and straightening furniture, they would race the little tricycles around the room, engage each other in crayon and eraser fights, and commandeer whatever they could reach in the small refrigerator through the door that was always chained shut.

They also spent a great deal of their time in the recreation center. "The rec" was the cornerstone of the social construction of the neighborhood. Inside were countless activities available to the neighborhood kids. Allowed few other options by his uncles, Mouse all but lived in the rec. And with Mouse, Tupac began to spend much of his time there as well.

Another favorite pastime of theirs was taking in a movie at the notorious Boulevard Theater, less than a mile down Greenmount Avenue. Most well known around the city for its, at times, tough patrons and no-frills accommodations, the Boulevard reached the height of its notoriety on a fatal evening in which a teenage boy was pushed through the glass of the front door and killed after a fight broke out in the crowded line outside. Tupac and Mouse were in the line that night, waiting to see, yet again, the popular hip-hop film *Beat Street*, which had drawn the unusually large crowd. Violence and death were something with which they were familiar.

They would attend numerous candlelight vigils for fallen peers in the few years of their time together in the neighborhood.

The following year, their first year of high school, Mouse went to the zone school for their neighborhood, Northern High, and Tupac to Paul Laurence Dunbar High, also a public school but one with some special programs that accepted students from outside of the zone. Apparently Ms. Shakur had determined it to have a little more to offer than Northern, and had Tupac enrolled. However, located in one of the poorer sections of the city (the lower east side), Dunbar was a typical public school, where the average student neither traveled nor pondered beyond their own downtrodden neighborhood, and Tupac hated it there. It hadn't even the smidgen of a feeling of freedom felt at Roland Park Middle. And he now had no crew, no homeboy with whom to occupy himself through the day. According to a classmate from that year, Tupac was completely disinterested, and sat quietly in the back of his classes, doodling listlessly in his notebook. That former classmate also recalls how Tupac's notebook was the messiest he had ever seen.

However the tone of his experience at the school changed dramatically with the beginning of the second semester. There was a talent contest. Of course he entered Mouse and himself, and of course they ripped up the stage. There were a number of student rap groups that performed that evening, so a certain standard had been laid down by the time they performed in the next to the last slot. A standard they smashed purposefully, trouncing with big cocky steps, not only hitting their rhymes with comfortable precision, but working the stage as they had learned to do in the months since their virgin experience at the Mantronix show. They easily won first place. The large crowd reacted to them as if they were celebrities. Everyone at the school would certainly know who Tupac was from that night on. Someone would even think enough of him to obtain and hold onto, for years, his school ID. That evening he and Mouse both went home with multiple phone numbers etched on various little pieces of paper crumpled up in their pockets.

Over the remainder of the year, guys would always want to battle and girls would jock. The challenges from the guys Tupac wisely refused, stating that the deed had been done and there was nothing for him to prove. Devoid of crew and far from home, he was in no position to engage in such confrontations, no shortage of which escalated into all-out throw-downs in those days, the losers eager to win some form of recourse.

After the pivotal evening, Tupac's reports back to Mouse of the school were much more involved, and told with interest. But he was definitely not returning the following year. There was a school downtown he had found out about that was like the one up in New York that his cousin Scott had attended for drama; and this was what he wanted without hesitation. He had been in a small production of *A Raisin in the Sun* with Scott a few years before. He enjoyed the experience so much that the future had been made clear to him: He would be an actor. With a select monologue from the play already committed to memory, he was ready for an audition at the Baltimore School for the Arts. There was no question in his mind whether he would be accepted.

Breaking the Ice

Following the lopsided battle, we wanted only to forget the whole thing, to act as if it had never happened; but the wounds to our egos were far too deep to be made over so easily. It would be some time before we would speak to our new nemesis again. Though his talent was undeniable and his charisma admirable, there would be no conceding the victory to him. We could do no such thing. Not only were our egos badly bruised, but at the hand of a younger student who seemed to revel in a cockiness that we all found unsettling.

Kendrick and Ernest would scarcely look at the newcomer in the days and weeks that followed. Zorian would avoid him wholeheartedly; his once frequent visits to the school decreased noticeably. They even took to talking badly about the now not-so-new guy whenever possible. That was their way, cracking on people, and tearing them down. That's what The Dozens had always been about, brothers and sisters cutting down brothers and sisters. I never saw any of the white kids cutting each other down like that. They would just gather around us and laugh, entertained by us going at each other. Ernest and those guys would get right hurtful with it. I didn't really vibe that way. Like Tupac, I, too, was from a poor family that neither could nor saw fit to afford the latest fashions, or even their better imitations, for that matter. Middle school for me had been a painful collage of teasing, insult, and embarrassment; my secondhand, marked-down nonfashions were totally unacceptable to the unforgiving teens and preteens. So I was uncomfortable with the biting nature of the commando rhyming employed in The Dozens. Plus I had acne, and a large forehead to boot. Hell no. I knew I represented an abundance of material for anyone mean enough to go there. So I was careful about my forays into The Dozens, and the rhymes I selected. And I was uncomfortable with the things the guys were saying about Tupac.

Seeing the ease with which Tupac moved among the white students of the school, Ernest began to say that he was "trying to be white." And he would always crack on his clothing, calling him "Bummy" and "Dirty." To the latter of these attempts at insult, I took offense, not finding them at all funny. I had gladly left my middle school experience far behind in the deeper reaches of memory. And hearing such things again kind of disgusted me. In fact I admired the impressive skill of our enemy more than I hated the sight of his face. I wished to go against him again some day, and beat him in all of his splendor, not ridicule or undermine him.

In the weeks that followed, I would see Tupac in the hallways, lunchroom, and around the school and barely speak a word to him. Again and again, I went over the scene of the colossal battle in my head, obsessing over it, revisiting in excruciating detail every nuance, every little ingredient that had contributed to his perfect performance. What stood out was the key role played by Mouse and the uncanny coordination between the two of them. I immediately set out in my own neighborhood to find comparable accompaniment. But this quickly proved to be quite unattainable. As I would later understand, Mouse was an extremely unusual talent at this popular, instrumentless form of percussion. The things Mouse could do with his vocal chords, the many sounds he could produce so clearly, simultaneously, was incredible. Unable to find even a close second, I enlisted a pair of twin brothers that lived down the street from me. Younger in age than I, they looked up to me, and were therefore open to being led around and instructed in whatever ways I saw fit. The novelty of this identical duo I found irresistible, and for a very short while even promising. As a tester I tried them out on Jada Pinkett, who was also a student at the Baltimore School for the Arts. She lived only a few blocks away from me, and thought they were just adorable. But even the two of them together I realized were no match for Mouse, and I all but gave up the search. Yet still I kept my eyes open, hopeful. Without an excellent beatbox, the coup could not be had.

Several weeks later as I walked through the halls in the basement of the school on my way to the cafeteria I heard noises coming from the locker rooms. Passing the doorway, I could hear what sounded like Tupac rapping over a beat provided by students beating on lockers and beatboxing. I decided to go in. Tupac was in there rapping off the top of his head, having fun with it, moving from side to side, really getting into it. He was surrounded by several other sophomores or freshmen whom I didn't really know, some white, some black. A couple of them were jumping in and giving it a go, but without much success. After I stood there listening for a minute, Tupac beckoned to me to join in. "Kick one," he said, looking at me, smiling, and waving me over to the circle. So I walked closer and kicked a little verse off the top of my head. He laughed in approval, and followed. We went back and forth a couple of times with the other kids just listening. We were breaking the ice. After that, when I would see him throughout the course of the school day, we would always speak, and he would ask me if I had written any new rhymes. I guess he just loved the fact that there were others in the school who shared his love for rap.

Midway through the school year was a time of coming together within the student body. Dismissals from the school occurred over the midyear and summer breaks. The midyear dismissals were much more noticeable and dramatic as they appeared to be more a cruel in-process ousting than a well-weighed difficult decision. There was great pressure on students to perform both artistically and academically; many did not make the cut. It was during this time that a group of us were seated around a table in the cafeteria. Kendrick and I were working on a new rhyme of ours, "Bitchy Bitches," when Tupac happened into the lunchroom, probably taking a break from one of his drama classes in the theater nearby. He saw us around the table rhyming and made his way over, then stood there listening. This was a few weeks after the cipher in the locker room where he and I had broken the ice; now it was time for him and everyone else in the crew to do so. I had paved the way for this to happen, telling everyone (namely Kendrick and Ernest) how cool Tupac really was. This was a moment we all had wanted for some time, and were quite relieved when it finally occurred. It was ridiculous for us to avoid each other in an environment so small.

When Tupac walked over to our table it was his way of saying, "I'm just like you guys . . . this whole *beef* thing is stupid." He wanted to get to know us as much as we wanted to know him. Still, I couldn't help but think that in the back of his mind, he knew he had already made his point at the Beaux Arts Ball. But he was obviously uncomfortable with his alienation from the few kids in the school who shared his truest passion. And he had never been fully accepted by the kids who, early on, congregated around him as friends. To them he was more novelty than comrade, his extraordinary and unique vibration far too foreign for them to assimilate with any degree of success; and he knew this all too well. As I would grow to know him better I would realize that this was nothing new to him. He seemed to be the type of guy who one either loved or hated, and I could find no valid reason to hate him, or even dislike him for that matter. He was simply different.

In the following weeks we all grew increasingly comfortable and familiar with each other. Before long Tupac was part of the crew, with all animosity left in the past. He now had the school sewn up from end to end, encompassing all circles and factions. Most importantly, he was now part of the rap crew; the king now had a kingdom.

 **Spring Fever**

The school put on an annual performance show called "Spring Fever," a showcase of student pieces for which all aspirants were required to audition. Again wanting a piece of the action, Gerard and I developed a dramatic skit in which much of the dialogue was conveyed through rap, a sort of hip-hop opera. The piece was entitled "I Wannabe Your Man," a classic tale of popular jock against nerd, this before the release of *Revenge of the Nerds*, the popular movie with the same premise. I enlisted Tupac to play the part of the class jock who always got the girl; in this role, he would certainly be an enthusiastic participant. I played the nerd, with eyeglasses, high-waters, and a shirt-pocket full of pens. The main gist of the story was my seemingly hopeless pursuit of Tupac's girl, over whom I eventually won an improbable victory on the merit of my heart-wrenching love poem, performed as a rap. Rounding out the cast was Gerard, a couple other guys, and a troupe of the prettiest girls from the dance department. We went into the audition full of enthusiasm, confident of the quality of our product, but were turned down despite what we all felt to be an excellent performance. Rap, at the time, was still looked down upon as a groundless fad, not to be taken seriously. And I knew that this was what I had seen behind the uninterested eyes of the judges. The following day of auditions, Tupac and Mouse performed a rap of theirs entitled "Babies Having Babies," a commentary on the rising problem of teen pregnancy, particularly poignant in Baltimore, which was among the nation's leaders at the time. Despite their excellent performance, this too was rejected, lending further support to my indictment of the judging process. But Tupac was determined and managed an appearance in the showcase by joining several other theater students in a skit taken from *A Raisin in the Sun*.

Following the auditions I made it a point to get to know Tupac and Mouse more intimately. Hearing their performance of "Babies Having Babies," I was introduced to a side of Tupac that I hadn't considered. I already admired his unusual skill and charisma, but my appreciation of him broadened. He wasn't all show, all "huff" and all "puff." He was actually saying something of civic importance, something he had obviously considered deeply.

And I began to realize that we actually held a lot in common as far as our backgrounds were concerned. We were both the eldest of two siblings in a one-parent household, our fathers no more than a question mark with barely a face to associate. And we both came from poor families, knowing well the lasting sting of embarrassment. The derogatory name-calling and trash-talking of my sorely beaten crew in the period following the battle only served to draw me closer to the focus of their animosity, providing me a peek behind the armor of this unbelievable rap talent, where he nursed a serious vulnerability with which I was very familiar and easily empathetic.

I began to wonder how he could be so strong and confident, and so effective as a rapper. I started to observe him closely, meticulously, looking for that thing that powered him. I've always felt that the biggest, most profound answers are often found in the smallest things, and we often miss them. Tupac, without question, had something special. And I wanted it, or at least as much of my version of it as I could produce. Although I was always extremely confident, and more than ready to face any challenge, much of my overt confidence was born from a certain insecurity, a sort of pre-emptive strike to keep adversaries away from my vulnerabilities and weaknesses. And though I felt that I was good at those things to which I set my mind, I never felt that I was exceptional. In rap, Tupac had clearly proven himself exceptional. And I was most curious and interested in exactly how he was able to achieve this so definitively.

My attempts to figure out my new subject were compromised by a veil that hovered about him, obscuring any possible clear view. One moment he was joking loudly and having fun, the next pensively quiet and still. He was at once the jokester busting provocative rhymes at the back of the bus, and, I had begun to notice, the quiet guy sneaking off to the library where he would often spend entire lunch periods. Not privy to such information at the time, I would later find out from Ms. Rogers, the school librarian, that he was always in the library, reading, in her estimation, "almost every book in there." She couldn't believe the amount that he read, and the range of the titles.

I would also realize that he often had no lunch money, and

retreated to the library in order to bury himself in stories and information, redirecting his thoughts from hunger, and avoiding the pity and spectacle of sitting among everyone in the lunchroom with neither lunch bag nor tray. He used to tell me how he liked to read stories, both fiction and nonfiction, and to fantasize about being someone other than himself, someone without all of the pain and trouble. I figured this was probably how he spent many of those hours by himself in the library.

Tupac's performance in the *Raisin in the Sun* skit at the Spring Fever show was impressive, but still I was more impressed with his rapping than I was with his acting. This may have been due to my own prejudices and to the fact that I had only seen him act on a couple of occasions; he didn't participate in any of the major school productions, the general rule for underclassmen. That's why it was kind of strange seeing him perform at the Spring Fever show, watching him up there in his element. I had known him as rapper extraordinaire, so talented, and so far above the rest that it didn't seem right for him to have yet another love and passion central to his life.

Under the lights up on stage he appeared a veteran, carefully delivering lines with measured power. The character that he portrayed in the skit, Walter Lee, was a young man who spoke passionately to his mother about his going out into the world and making something of himself. The passion and anger summoned during this shirtless portrayal seemed to flow from within him naturally, making me consider the real life source from which he seemed to draw without fear of any perceived bottom. I began to wonder about the other half of his life, his life at home, his family life.

I knew little more about Tupac's life outside of school than the obvious: He was from New York, and he was obsessed with rap. He was boundlessly proud of his New York roots. He used his New Yorkness strategically, always playing it out with a certain bravado, in whatever he was doing. He liked to season this presented figure of himself with mannerisms and styles of speaking borrowed from his biggest idol, the quintessential New York figure, LL Cool J. Like this equally confident idol of his, Tupac insisted on being the best. Either you were the best, or you were nobody as far as he was concerned; there was no in-between. I really admired this about him. Prior to my meeting Tupac I had thought of myself as having quite a large ego, but his was a person in and of itself, its own entity. I would wonder how and why he had become so confident. Certainly there were answers to this question in the home and in the family. But other than seeing his mother once after school when she had come up for a meeting, this remained a mystery to me for quite some time. However, I would soon gain this coveted look inside for which I had waited since the night of the Beaux Arts Ball at the beginning of the year.

One day, not long after Spring Fever (dubbed "The Jada Pinkett Show" that year because she took part in five of the entries), Kendrick and I were walking with Tupac out the front door after school when we noticed six brothers standing idly across the street. They were dressed in the typical apparel—jeans, tennis shoes, T-shirts, baseball caps—and were looking intently at us as if they had trouble on their minds. Occasionally, guys from other schools around the city would come down to ours to play tough guy for a day in front of the cute girls of the school. We were not known for having the toughest guys, and many young, urban opportunists would take advantage of this from time to time. As one of the guys, the biggest of the group, rose to his feet, I figured this was such a case; but something didn't seem right. It was pretty late after school and the front was all but empty. I looked around to Tupac, who was frozen in place, eyes trained on the guy now crossing the street. He said nothing but it seemed as though he knew something we did not. This big guy, I would later find out, was Avra's boyfriend. Avra was a theater student, an attractive white girl from the nicer side of Baltimore society who was known for her interest in Black guys, particularly those of the rougher, inner-city genus. She had taken a liking to Tupac, who returned her interest in kind, without regard for her supposedly tough and jealous boyfriend, a kid from a noto-riously rough public school on the edge of the city.

The stocky, intimidating looking guy walked right up to us. We braced ourselves. "Who's Tupac?" he said in a cold voice.

"I'm Tupac," Tupac replied defiantly. Without saying another word or wasting an instant, the guy swung and hit Tupac in the face, but managed no real damage. Tupac surged instantly back at him, swinging with everything he had, overwhelming the consider-ably bigger guy. In another instant they were on the ground with Tupac on top of him swinging wildly but connecting all the same. The instigator of the whole thing, the boyfriend, then ran across the street and began to pull Tupac off of his buddy. Kendrick and I immediately grabbed him and pulled him off of Tupac, at which time the security guard and others came running out the front door. The other four guys never did venture across the street. I guess they weren't so tough after all.

After several minutes of posturing, a lame attempt at saving face, the would-be tough guys walked off less than proudly, their intended beat-down a dismal failure. Neither Tupac's pride nor person had been damaged in any way. I was a little shocked. I would never have expected so strong a showing of heart from the rapper/ actor had I time to consider the outcome beforehand. Heart like that was rare. And this new friend of mine had never shown any indication that he had such heart to wield outside of the sheltered school environment and immaterial world of rhyming and drama, heart to maintain a posture of strength and perseverance in the face of real violent confrontation. I was bigger than he was, and had always been one of the crazier scrappers in my neighborhood when provoked, and I had been a little taken aback by the size of the attacker. Tupac showed me something that day that only impressed me further.

Still intensely pumped up, with adrenaline-saturated blood racing through our veins, we firmly clasped hands with those around us. Tupac offered several thank you's for the support he had received. He gave me a look in the eyes that effectively communicated what probably would have sounded awkward in words. With nothing left to do but go home, he and I offered our slightly dazed and numb good-byes to all of those still out front and walked off.

He was furious, and began to engage me in one of those conversations of the uninterruptible sort. We were headed toward his stop; I was following. "Yo, that nigga ain't even show up," he said, with deep hurt in his eyes. I was confused. "My *man* was supposed to be there and ain't even show up." That's when I realized that he had been expecting trouble. Avra must have warned him ahead of time. "Niggas I don't even know was there for me and my *man* ain't even show up. That's fucked up!" he yelled to the street before him. His "man" he was talking about was Mouse. "You was there. Yo . . . Thanks . . ."

The conversation continued in this manner up until the arrival of the bus and through the entire ride. "You comin' over right?" he had asked as the bus pulled to the curb before us. I just nodded my head, quietly excited to finally see what was behind this strange kid. What had made him what he was? What was empowering him to become what he was becoming?

After thirty minutes on the bus, he grabbed the cord signaling the driver, and the bus pulled over on Greenmount Avenue less than a mile above 33rd Street. The infamous north-south thoroughfare, particularly the two-mile stretch from North Avenue to Coldspring Lane, at the center of which was 33rd Street, was the setting for some of the most publicized shootings of that period. The stretch of the avenue that lay above 33rd Street, with its well-aged houses, towering bushes, and patchy, unmanicured lawns, had always intrigued me. It seemed to be some kind of no-man's land beyond the busy commercial block where the Boulevard Theater on one corner, a gas station on the other, and shops and restaurants all around, lit up the area. Whether on my way to the stadium, farther east along 33rd Street, or some other Northeast Baltimore destination, I had taken note of the stretch of Greenmount Avenue enough times to remember doing so when I first traveled up it two years before on my way to Gerard's house, which was farther up, off another, very different section of the avenue. Having pulled his things together, Tupac walked off the bus and I followed.

3955 Greenmount Avenue

After stepping off the bus we took just a few more steps before hopping up the front stoop of the first floor apartment directly in front of the stop. "He's *right on* the strip!" I remember thinking, a little surprised. The apartment was the bottom half of an old two-story row house that had been converted into two separate units. Walking through the front door I was immediately humbled by the sight. There was very little inside. The few things there were inside were arranged tidily.

Since being given the choice, a few years back, to move in with my grandmother, and jumping immediately at the chance, I had lived in relative comfort, far removed from what I saw before me. But I definitely knew a little something about this way of life, where I used my rank over my younger brother to secure the top bunk in order to evade aggressive rats that thought they owned the place after dark. In fact, my first thought upon entering the apartment was that it reminded me very much of the last apartment I lived in with my mother.

The skinny apartment stretched down the length of the front door hallway to a closed door at the end, with a couple rooms branching off to the right. The rooms were not conventional rooms, just space broken up into areas to be used differently at different times. The largest room at the front of the apartment functioned as the living room, while the next room down the hallway was both the dining room and a sleeping area. Tupac introduced me to his younger sister, Setchua, in what was, at that hour, the living room. He allowed for little more than the standard formal word before ushering me on to the back. At the end of the hall we stepped into a small dark room that seemed to me a pantry, where Ms. Shakur lay resting on the well broken-in mattress of a small single bed.

"Ma, this is Darrin," Tupac introduced me as she looked up to us. "He had my back today when them boys tried to bank me!" He added this with intentional fervor, as if there were an underlying meaning of which they were both perfectly aware, and which he had learned from her. To this her eyes opened widely and she took a good look at me. "Mouse ain't even show up, Ma," he added with disgust.

"Really," she replied, taking on a stern expression. Tupac said a few more words as she sat up, looking through me with a stare that burned. She took my hand. I was immediately accepted as family without pomp or pretense, two things that obviously did not exist within this family.

Before we sank any further into small talk, Ms. Shakur produced ten dollars and told Tupac to run out and fetch her a sack. This shocked and bewildered me, but I said nothing, making sure to show no reaction. Stunned, I followed Tupac out of the room. "Nice to meet you, Ms. Shakur," I was able to say by reflex before leaving in a cloud of confusion.

Far from one of the more experimental, experienced brothers in Baltimore City, I was a kid who knew what was right and what was wrong; and drugs were wrong. I may not have liked Ronald Reagan, but certainly Nancy was virtuous in espousing "Just Say No." And that's what I did around my neighborhood or wherever else I may have been confronted with such substances. I always saw myself as a positive young man, as one of the positive exceptions in an environment filled with negativity and misfortune. In "Gifted and Talented Education (GATE)" programs throughout elementary school, I was all about being talented, and being positive. Drugs struck me as the epitome of negativity. You can imagine the perplexity that I felt, too much to utter a word.

We walked back out the front door and onto Greenmount Avenue. Walking down the block, Tupac casually asked a couple people as to the whereabouts of some guy whom they hadn't seen. They suggested he might be "up top," up by the neighborhood store that was on the other side of the playground behind his place, a block off Greenmount. We continued around the corner in this direction when Tupac spotted an older, heavyset guy hanging out in front of a house halfway up the street. "There's his uncle," he said to me, leading the way over to the guy. When we walked up to the guy Tupac greeted him with a "W'sup," and a hard handclasp. "Where's your nephew at?" he asked the guy. "I'm tryin' to see'm." I just stood off a slight distance.

"Oh, you can see me for that," the guy replied casually, directing Tupac down the street where he would meet up with him, and then walked off in the opposite direction. Tupac and I headed down the street. In no time the guy reappeared from behind the houses and met up with us. They again clasped hands and said a few more words. The guy smilingly made a comment about Tupac's rapping. "I like that shit you hit last time," he said, again smacking Tupac's hand, this time in recognition. "That shit was *on time*." Tupac smiled widely as he took the guy's hand. I could tell he thoroughly enjoyed the compliment. We then walked off, a few steps after which it occurred to me that in the mix of the conversation they had forgotten the very thing for which we came out in the first place.

"Yo, you forgot about the shit," I told him, laughing, proud of my own presence of mind.

"No I didn't. I got it in my pocket," he replied.

"Ohhh . . . Yeah, that's right." I tried to play it off, acting as if there was something I had just remembered.

Without missing a beat he went on about the drug dealers in the area, and how they all liked to hear him rap and would give him money just to do so. As he talked I listened with only half of my attention. The other half was still dealing with the phantom transaction, busily reviewing the scene over and over. I finally figured they must have made the exchange within a handshake. It had completely escaped my notice.

We walked back to the playground behind his apartment and sat on the little climbing structure in the middle. Finally having a chance to explore the craziness of this little venture of ours, I brought it up for discussion. Before the extraordinary events of the previous half hour, I wouldn't have thought for a second that my new friend smoked pot, let alone that his mother did, or that it was a common and accepted thing, so much so that she would even have him fetch her a sack! It was all quite unconscionable to me. I tried to imagine my mother doing the same, and couldn't manage the picture in my mind. I was *really* thrown off balance when he told me they smoked together on occasion. What?!

And they discussed everything? There was no topic considered taboo. Ms. Shakur was in no way a bashful lady, and, as with anyone else she encountered, there was nothing about which she was scared to talk with her children. It was becoming clear to me how this mysterious new friend of mine had gotten to be so mature at such a young age. I began to feel as if there was a whole other side of life out there to which I had never been exposed, and about which I was learning from him.

Still in the playground, now atop the upper level of the climbing structure, he began to tell me about an event he was putting together in the neighborhood for a friend who had been shot and killed. The boy's name was Darren Barret. I found this a little eerie since the boy and I shared the same first name and initials. The event would be called "In Candlelight Memory of Darren Barret." This was a relatively large project and I could see in his eyes that it meant a great deal to him. Apparently Darren Barret, known in the neighborhood as "Snoop," had been an influential character to Tupac. A couple of years older than Tupac and Mouse and one of the more charismatic boys in the neighborhood, Snoop was well liked, and more importantly, had never had a problem with Tupac (one of the few such cases in the neighborhood). Tupac looked up to the flashy, in ways eccentric, older hustler. And it was from Snoop that Tupac borrowed his habit of coming out of his shirt at the drop of a dime, whenever at all possible. Snoop was known for this around the neighborhood, always taking off his shirt, tearing through one in the middle of the basketball court during a game just like when David Banner turned into the Incredible Hulk; and even cutting holes in brand-new ones just for the aesthetic. Anything to show-case his chiseled torso. Tupac took death of this flamboyant older supporter of his to heart.

Although he would continue to attend numerous candlelight services throughout his years in the neighborhood, this one was a little different. And he wanted to help make it so, not only helping to organize the whole thing, but also performing. The tenth-grader put his full energy into the memorial event, writing up and passing out fliers all over the neighborhood. He even went so far as to plaster the school with the materials as well, though I'm certain none of the students ventured even a thought of showing their standout faces at the Greenmount Avenue event. But Tupac was not just going through the motions, he was serious and adamant in his lobbying for students to show up and pay their respects to this important young life that had quietly meant more to him than people would probably suspect. He approached the advertising campaign like a grassroots activist, as if he wished to facilitate a greater discussion on the senselessness of the out-of-control killing of young boys in the inner city.

Tupac understood the significance of the similarities between him and Snoop as two young, underprivileged boys in the same neighborhood, growing up under many of the same circumstances. The fate that had befallen this friend of his made him consider his own. The tribute could easily be seen as one to his own feeling of self-worth and right to live and experience, as it could one to that of his tragically denied, slain comrade. The memorial turned out to be a huge success, well attended by everyone in the area. For this he received a lot of respect in the neighborhood, which meant more to him than anything. He was exceedingly proud of the accomplishment.

After twenty minutes or so of talking in the playground, we returned to the house. Tupac went straight back to the room in which
his mother was resting. I waited by the kitchen. When he came
out, he led me into the kitchen and started rummaging through the
cupboards. Dutifully, he pulled out a couple packs of Oodles of
Noodles, then a pot from under the sink, and started filling the pot
with water. He didn't even ask if I was hungry. It was kind of like a
basic sustenance, primal thing: you've been at school, now you're
home, now we restore the vital energy that's been lost, we eat.
When we finished the noodles we went back out the front door and
sat on the stoop. He began to talk about his mother and various
things of note from his past.

"What's a Black Panther?" I asked, eyebrows furrowed, face
scrunched up when he told me his mother was a member.

"You never heard of the Black Panthers?" He said this with a
touch of surprise, more a conscious maneuver placing the organization about which he was going to tell me in a certain light, than it
was a true expression of the emotion. While considerably more
could be expected of the average kid in New York City, this was his
third year in Baltimore, and he was well aware of the cluelessness.
He was finally able to make a connection in my head by referencing
the school breakfast programs that were their creation. To this I
could reply with familiarity as my brother and I had taken part in
such a program in elementary school. I exaggerated the extent to
which the revelation opened my eyes to the reality behind it. Beginning to feel ashamed of my complete ignorance of all that he
was telling me about the accomplishments of the organization, and
its intensely controversial position in the politics of the country, I
was happy to find some way to appear at least somewhat knowledgeable. He went on to recount a ready-made list of certain heroic

deeds of his mother's, and how unbelievable forces would regularly swoop down on their fragile world to breed havoc and chaos. They—the nameless, faceless conglomerate of governmental, police, landlord, and whatever other forces that regularly interfered in their lives—had even tried to burn down his house. I was awestruck. "They set your shit on *fire*?!" I asked, amazed. I could hardly believe what I was hearing. It all sounded like some kind of far-out stuff from some movie to me.

When we went back inside, Tupac led me into the living room area, where he proudly drew my attention to his wall of awards. Again I was awestruck. There were countless awards, certificates, and trophies set atop the mantlepiece (under which there was no fireplace) and all over the wall. All of them for rap and all of them showing first place. Apparently no second- or third-place acknowledgment ever defiled the die-hard, utopian vision given voice through this conspicuously arrayed and disconcertingly impressive wall. I was blown away. One of the earliest dates I noticed belonged to his first-place award from a rap contest sponsored by the Enoch Pratt Free Library in 1985. I would later find out from Ms. Taylor, the organizer of the event, that despite a preponderance of solid, well-crafted written entries, among which there was little difference, Tupac and Mouse proved to be "far and away the best" when the live performances were offered.

Ms. Shakur came out to the living room, looking very different from the woman to whom I had been introduced just a short while earlier. Smilingly she engaged us in conversation, obviously enjoying the opportunity to express her pride for her baby; she also seemed to take pleasure in my new presence and the hallowed opportunity it provided, allowing her to plant fresh new seeds. "I always tell Tupac that if you're going to do anything, make sure you do your best and never settle for less," she said, directing her words to me from behind, also admiring the impressive display. She spoke of how one must keep pushing, how the attainment of the goal is then but an eventuality. This powerful, radiant woman addressing me, erect and proud in the light of day, was not at all the figure I had seen laying crumpled in the small dark bed, awaiting the return of her sack of sedation. She was strong and bounding with life, almost otherworldly.

In my family it had always been my grandmother who backed me. My mother was more of a sideline presence. So I found this relationship between Tupac and his mother particularly enlightening. Hanging out at Gerard's, in his middle class neighborhood with his hardworking mother and father, the ideal I had attempted to force on my own dysfunctional family life was simply unattainable, not even applicable. But at Tupac's I witnessed a single-parent, greatly impoverished family scenario that was still powerfully positive. Eager to fill the void in my life left by an unknown father and a strained relationship with my mother, I had developed a very close relationship with Gerard's parents, and borrowed a great deal of guidance and advice from them. Now I was listening intently to this single mom who was very different from the single mother prototype with which I was intimately familiar. Again I was taking advantage of the parental presence of a friend more fortunate than myself. It is ironic to speak of Tupac being somehow fortunate in terms of his family situation, but with respect to the wisdom and awareness of his mother, Tupac was unusually fortunate.

Tupac and his mother communicated openly and unashamedly; that's why he wasn't afraid to express himself. The once intriguingly, even mystically blurred picture was becoming more and more clear. Ms. Shakur spoke like a prophet with her words of wisdom and sobering perspectives on reality. She was the burning fire behind his red-hot personality and the guiding light leading him to question, always more deeply, in his times of quiet contemplation. She meant everything to him.

When I was finished with "the wall" Ms. Shakur asked me about myself. Carefully she listened to every word as I responded. She said nothing negative or at all condescending. There was no pessimism or parental overbearing in her words. She offered only strong encouragement, telling me to fearlessly pursue my dreams until fulfillment. There was raw truth in her eyes and a calming warmth about her person. It ignited in me a certain feeling of bliss and belonging the way she spoke to me as if I were her very own, this amazingly strong woman. I felt like family.

A Revolutionary

Although Tupac centered his life around what was at that time considered a fad, it was not merely for fun, for laughs and accolades. When Tupac recited a line, you knew he meant it. Even the simplest line you could just tell was deeply considered and thoroughly planned. It was the feeling and the conviction behind his delivery as much as anything else that set his stuff apart. He had strong opinions, real feelings about the real things around him. He was an activist by nature, and his rhymes followed suit. Born to a notorious Black Panther at the climax of her infamous sojourn across the national stage, Tupac came into the world a child of controversy and political upheaval. His introduction to society was one of police harassment, mysterious fires, and questionable imprisonment, even assassination, of elder acquaintances. One of the closest of these acquaintances was Tupac's godfather, Geronimo Pratt, a famed political prisoner framed by the Oakland and Los Angeles police forces, and imprisoned in 1972, only to be released and fully exonerated of all charges over twenty years later under intense international pressure. For a young Tupac, the unjust nature of his country was well understood, and the need for solution a given. He did not have to be coaxed onto the political stage. It was in his very construction.

Growing up under the tutelage of an activist mother and her equally forthright and informed friends who believed in hiding nothing from her son, a very young Tupac already carried with him what most young social detractors do not acquire until bitten by the bug of discovery and social rebellion incumbent to some particularly conscious experience, usually their first year of college. When at ten years of age he was asked by a family friend what he wanted to be when he grew up, his reply was, "a revolutionary." But more than the simple product of the activist culture in which he was raised, Tupac possessed an innate and unyielding understanding of justice, and was stubbornly intolerant of anything less. As with his defiant stand against the much bigger Fat Will on his first day at Roland Park Middle School, purely on the grounds that he had been given lawful sanction to take the seat, he simply did not know how to be quiet, or impassive.

In high school Tupac began to formalize his politics, and actively participated in several grassroots organizations to which he gave his full energy and creativity. He would speak of the activities of these organizations freely, occasionally sporting related buttons on his clothing and showcasing various leaflets, flyers, and other written material. A number of us from the school found ourselves at meetings on more than one occasion.

The first of Tupac's organizational affiliations was with the "Yo-

No" anti–gun violence campaign of the North East Community Organization, known as NECO among other participating organizations, led by community activist Truxon Sykes. Truxon was the lead organizer on several fronts of the multidimensional battle waged by the impoverished community against the forces both encroaching upon it and festering within. As an ex-addict, he was a substance abuse counselor. He ran the very powerful NECO, which is, to this day, the oldest nonprofit community activist organization in Maryland. Under Truxon's leadership NECO successfully blocked the opening of numerous liquor stores, making theirs the only lower middle-class to poor Black community in the city in which one can drive for blocks and not see even one. Truxon also started the Baltimore Homeless Union, which fed over 60,000 families and organized over 10,000 homeless persons in registering to vote in Baltimore City.

Tupac became familiar with the controversial activist through his little sister, Setchua. Soon after the family's arrival in Baltimore, Setchua developed a close friendship with a girl in the neighborhood with whom she would spend much of her time. Often she would remain over the girl's house until dark, in which case Tupac would be sent to pick her up and walk her home. As a result of the subtle prodding of his mother as well as his own intensely protective nature, Tupac would curiously survey the unfamiliar home on these occasions, engaging the girl's "father" (really her guardian) in conversation. This guardian turned out to be Truxon Sykes. He was taking care of the girl as his own in the absence of her mother, who never returned after leaving her with the community leader for "a couple of hours" over two years before. A curiously well-informed and experienced older leader, Truxon proved to be an intriguing character to whom Tupac took immediately. Never did Truxon speak down to the lively young boy as some poorly comprehending, unworthy younger intellect, but intelligently, as a young man with all expected cognitive ability. Tupac would become absorbed with the endless information, and ask for more. They did not talk about drugs in clichéd and meaningless political speak, but as business's and political leadership's primary tool of gentrification in poor Black neighborhoods. Tupac learned how the property was allowed to devalue so that more affluent business owners and residents could move in at pennies to the dollar before renovation initiatives were launched, and how the police were only happy enough to exploit this understood disregard, collecting a cut from the covertly sanctioned drug dealing enterprises without fear of reprisal.

When Truxon started through his organization the "Yo-No" anti–gun violence campaign, Tupac and his girlfriend at the time, Mary Baldridge, got deeply involved. Mary was a white girl in the dance department with an exceptional body that most of the Black guys at the school agreed was impressive. But it was as much Mary's upbringing and family orientation that facilitated her and Tupac's relationship as it was her impressive physique. Mary's parents were open-minded, activist types who were fond of Tupac and supportive of the young couple's activities. I was initially suspicious of Mary, and the degree of her understanding of her boyfriend, and the sincerity of her interest in him. But when I visited her house and met some of her friends outside of school, and her family, I saw that her reality was one of people as people, and not one of some people as novelty, as I seemed to find with many persons of privilege. I also saw that her family genuinely saw something special in their daughter's charismatic boyfriend.

Tupac and Mary were quite the activist couple. In support of the "Yo-No" campaign, the two went out into the community and canvassed homes door to door, informing residents of issues and pertinent meetings. They even wrote a half-hour operetta dealing with the issues of teen pregnancy and gun violence, and traveled to several churches and schools around town to perform the impressive production, which involved no less than six players. Tupac would also write raps for the organizational rallies, many of which were cooperative events contributed to by several organizations including the NAACP youth organization.

At one of the meetings held during the "Yo-No" campaign, Tupac stood up and spoke on the importance of opportunity. Particularly impressive to those in attendance was the captivating manner in which he drove home his point by citing his own experience, explaining with intimate candor the life-altering significance of the opportunity afforded him through his acceptance into the Baltimore School for the Arts. At the unique school he benefited immeasurably from a new and different environment thick with the themes of confidence, aspiration, and inclusion, far removed from the directionless, self-doubting self-destructiveness of the ghetto. Without it, he told the group, he would certainly have been but another statistic in the tragically long list, another faceless name, the mere difference between 101 and 102 in that year's murder tally.

Tupac and Mary were also closely involved with the Young Communist League (YCL). Mary's father was the director of the Communist Party in Baltimore, so she had been active in the organization for some time. For Tupac the organization was no hard sell. Having suffered his entire life under the painful grip of extreme poverty, he found their economic and social philosophies appealing. The idea of dissolving the deeply entrenched lines of economic class in America, and of proactively including all Americans in a more equitable division of the fruits of their own labor, was one he easily supported. With equal dedication, they lent their artistic talents to this organization as well, developing plays and skits. As unabashed ambassadors they made sure to bring as many School for the Arts students to the meetings as possible, myself among them on several occasions.

Tupac also got involved in the heated mayoral race that polarized the city in 1988, his junior year. For the first time in its history the predominantly Black city would have a Black mayor. Of the two leading candidates, one was the undereducated, hand-picked successor of the departing white incumbent, and the other, a polished Rhodes scholar and incumbent state's attorney. Not only was Tupac naturally suspicious of the former's connection to the departing administration, but the son of the latter was a student at the School for the Arts and a close friend. In support of his preferred candidate, the eventual winner of the contest, Tupac organized a rally on the neighborhood playground during which he and Mouse performed. The activist drive and ambition was as big a constituent in Tupac's blood as DNA, and his love for performing provided the perfect outlet.

 **Building Friendships**

Whenever I would see Tupac around school, his first words to me were always the same: "Write any new raps?" It was our connection to one another. We were steadily becoming closer, hanging out more and sharing mutual friends throughout the different social circles. Now in his second year at the school, Tupac was well removed from the limiting distinction of "new guy," having attained a wide ranging popularity. In fact, he had become a bona fide school personality. He was no longer, if he had ever been at the School for the Arts, "the skinny guy with the funny name," as he often referred to himself. Everyone, including me, was drawn to his confidence, to the exuberant energy that he brought to an inspired pursuit of the things that he loved. He was just so talented, so driven. The girls of the school considered him cute, and he had developed quite a repu tation as a ladies' man, sporting a new girlfriend almost every other month. But these girls were almost exclusively white. The Black girls were not so interested in Tupac. They couldn't get past his being so poor. And as the strong spell of Black self-hate still clung stubbornly in the minds of the sadly affected Black populace of the eighties, "light-skinned" was all the rage. Even the sistas who *were* caught under the equally powerful charm and charisma of this dark-skinned ghetto kid did their best to deny it. They were becoming increasingly curious, to the point that several of the normally stuck-up, "hard to get" sistas eventually satisfied their curiosity, including one quiet tryst in the school elevator, and at least one other in the locker rooms in the basement, but none of these girls ever admitted any such involvement with him. In fact, they generally denied it unequivocally. Such were the eighties. This must have hurt Tupac, to be publicly disowned this way. But he was undaunted. He figured he was getting what he wanted.

Tupac added to his mystique around school by developing a close friendship with a well-established recent ex-student, a former classmate of mine in the visual art department named John Cole, who was known as the cool white boy of the school. In contrast to Tupac's smooth, yet impoverished inner-city, "intelligent hoodlum" character, John was a polished, ivory pale-skinned and blue-eyed gentlemanly type, with long, thin blond hair and all of the right things to say. I called them the "Fuck Squad," which Tupac found hilarious. He told me that my use of the term made him envision himself "leading a squad of sex maniacs."

Tupac and John were spending a lot of time together, having met through Jada, who was one of Tupac's closer friends in the school and who was dating John at the time. Jada's close association to Tupac also played an instrumental role in his rise in the school. She having long since won a high seat in its social court on the merit of

Tupac during sophomore year in 1986
(Courtesy of the author)

Tupac and Mouse in New York in 1987
(Courtesy of Dana H. Smith)

y grandmother and I at her house in 1987
(Courtesy of the author)

sha Moses and I at the Junior Prom in 1987
(Courtesy of the author)

Gerard Young as a Visual Arts
student in 1988 (Courtesy of the author)

Darrin Bastfield—senior year at
Baltimore School of the Arts in 1988
(Courtesy of the author)

Tupac on the phone at John's house in 1988
(Courtesy of John Cole)

raduation barbecue at Gerard's house in 1988

Top to bottom: Gerard at the turntables; Tupac grooving with his headphones on; me and Tupac posing with the crew; Tupac dancing with two unidentified girls (Courtesy of Gerard Young [Ge-ology])

erard Young, Tupac Shakur, and I in 1988
(Courtesy of Tamara Payne)

her striking looks and hungry persona, equaled that of her ex-
traverted friend from New York, by way of East Baltimore. Similarly bold and forthright in their step, the two uniquely strong
personalities were immediately drawn to one another. It was obvious to me that Tupac liked Jada. But for whatever reasons, including the fact that she was going out with one of his best friends
through much of their friendship, Jada always seemed to be well
beyond his grasp, so he always spoke of her like a sister, and treated
her as such. Many of Tupac's new acquaintances he met through
Jada, and it was through her that he and John became exceptionally
close.

At home Tupac was in the midst of a deepening difficulty. His
mother's substance abuse went well beyond marijuana, and was becoming increasingly noticeable in the daily affairs of the home.
Laden with a growing responsibility and heightened level of household stress, the sixteen-year-old found himself pushed, more and
more, into the position of man of a household that lay upon treacherously shaky foundation, an undeniably daunting and troublesome
position, fraught with pitfalls. Combined with this increasing responsibility, Tupac was witnessing and experiencing over at John's
an enviable degree of freedom. And he wanted the same freedom at
home, freedom that his mother was unwilling to surrender. In John
and that other world in which John was deeply entrenched, he saw
an escape, and escape is what he did.

Situated not far from the school in the neighboring community
of Bolton Hill, a white upper middle-class neighborhood with
a "Bohemian" mood, John's house was something of a meeting
ground for many of the older students and other friends from
around town. With deep breaths of relief, well distanced and free
from the sullen-faced oppressiveness of Greenmount Avenue and

his dark little cubbyhole therein devoid of the most basic provision from front door to back, Tupac became a fixture over at John's house. It was like one big ongoing party over there; a seemingly endless stream of people were always present. There was plenty of food and drink and herb, not to mention clean clothes, matching towels and washcloths, nice sheets, nice furniture, new stereo, cable TV, etc. Since they had plenty anyway, and were not the type to be easily shocked or at all miserly, John's mother and stepfather accepted this unsanctioned, unofficial presence amiably, and Tupac easily made himself comfortable. In no time he carried himself around the home as if it were his own, with all privileges granted. I also hung out with them over at John's house for the same reasons, not just to chill with buddies, but to experience that previously unknown degree of freedom, that previously unknown degree of what I felt was luxury and comfort.

However, I quickly saw that all was not so rosy at John's house. I found out that white people had problems too, that although they seemed to have everything they could ever want, they were far from being as happy in the home as I had envisioned. Like Tupac and me, John also had never known his biological father. And this seemed to be at the root of some obvious tension between him and his stepfather. Additionally, John's mother was experiencing serious health problems, which further jumbled his already troubled teenage mind, and worsened the strain on his relationship with his parents. John was in rebellion. Some of the freedoms we enjoyed at his house were not necessarily sanctioned by his parents, but were pieces of a provocative line drawn in the sand which they did not have the energy or resolve to cross.

I saw this firsthand one morning after I stayed overnight. Tupac and I went to the kitchen to cook up some Steakum sandwiches. He rationed the number of Steakums I was allowed as if they were his own (himself one more than I), and comfortably went about pulling out pans and plates, pouring oil, and mustering up a loud and spattering frying frenzy. As the first Steakums crackled loudly in the greasy pan, John's stepfather stepped into the kitchen doorway and hesitated a moment before speaking.

"Good morning, Tupac," he said without expression, sounding not stunned but definitely taken aback. I could hear it in his voice, and I knew Tupac could hear it as well. I was in the far corner sitting down, beyond direct eye contact, but I'm sure my presence did not go unnoticed. My heart pounded uncomfortably in the silence that followed. Where I came from, what we were doing, you just didn't do in someone's home, especially when the man of the house was around. Certainly, John should have been with us in the kitchen; but he wasn't, his absence probably yet another intentional provocation. But Tupac was not swayed. I'll never forget the expression that came over his face. It was the exact same one he would later employ in his role in the movie *Juice*, looking across the crowded elevator at his costar and would-be murder victim Omar Epps, an expression I would notice on numerous occasions throughout our acquaintance. Blank and distant, disconnected in every way from the situation around him, as if it simply did not exist, he offered the standard response: "Good morning," barely looking up from the task at hand. John's stepfather left as quietly as he had come, and we completed and devoured our sandwiches.

Having come up his entire life with little more than absolutely nothing, and badly maligned for it, Tupac was a kid very much ready to receive when he came across someone willing and able to give, something like a benefactor. He had never had a friend like John before. As Mouse put it: "I mean, John was a white boy, so he had *benefits* . . . that niggas didn't have. He could have wild parties every night, in a phat-ass crib. He got food, got weed, got a car . . ." The environment over at John's was ripe for Tupac to not only live comfortably for once, but to drown himself in new stimuli, numbing the concern for his mother and little sister that weighed heavy on his consciousness. All of the girls, rabble-rousing and cavorting of that period were largely a diversion, a self-imposed smokescreen. It was just another surreal time for him in the unbroken chain.

Not only did Tupac make good use of what John had to offer, and further explore himself by way of the new experiences and perspectives he encountered, but John too borrowed and benefited from Tupac. Tupac was candid where John was guarded, assertive where John was reserved. The two fed off each other. When John's mother's condition worsened and she entered a coma, the two friends became even closer. John was going through a very difficult time and appreciated Tupac's support.

In October everyone geared up again for the Beaux Arts Ball, anticipating a rap battle; but this time it was the ladies' turn. They had witnessed the spectacle of the previous year and wanted a piece. Among those taking more interest were a number of girls, mostly of the Jada Pinkett sort, the largely "light-skinned," more popular girls of the school. Our informal contests had become high profile events in the school culture and these high profile girls naturally took part, becoming regular contributors and combatants. To this developing trend the other sistas in the school, the largely "dark-skinned," not particularly popular girls from rough neighborhoods like Edmonson Village and Cherry Hill, took exception, feeling that on top of their already being snubbed in so many ways at the school, they were being further disenfranchised by these girls of privilege who were now venturing into their very own backyard, and attempting to dispossess them of what little they could still claim as their own. Hip-hop was *their* culture, as far as they were concerned, a culture of the hard and dark inner-city streets and not the "well-to-do," manicured neighborhoods of these little high society girls who they felt didn't have a clue. Headed by Joyce Simms, a few of these disgruntled girls approached Jada and Jada's homegirl Linda, similarly to how Tupac had done Zorian and myself the year before, and laid down the challenge. Not the type to be intimidated, Jada and Linda duly accepted this challenge and again we were headed for a showdown at the Beaux Arts Ball.

I was closer friends with Jada than the other girls, so when I got word of the challenge, I set about conceptualizing a rhyme for her and Linda to use. Tupac did the same. I guess Joyce and her crew had a legitimate gripe after all. Once my idea was sufficiently developed I ran it by Jada, who agreed that it was good. I immediately got to work. The resulting piece was a sassy and funny rhyme entitled "You're a Hot Bitch," which I completed in one night of work. The following day I recited the new rhyme to Tupac, Jada, and a couple other students in the theater department workshop; they all liked it. Tupac gave me my props and Jada told me she definitely wanted to use it. She started practicing it with me right then and there. In the weeks afterward she, Linda, and I worked together so that they could learn the rhyme and get their delivery down pat. On a couple occasions I even went over to Jada's house just up the street from mine to further practice the piece.

The ball itself was a particularly funny affair that year. Tupac stepped into the dimmed light of the regal ballroom, under its vaulted ceilings decorated with ornate tapestry and multiple rich-looking chandeliers, wearing only a pair of leopard print bikini underwear, with a spear, and his roommate John in tow at the end of a leash. He was Shaka Zulu and John his white slave; a daring ensemble for which he won best costume. Everyone in the place tripped off of his incredible boldness. Once again, he was the immodest exhibitionist, grabbing any and every chance to show off his sleek body.

Mouse was also there that night, now a familiar face on the scene after he and Tupac's celebrated emergence exactly one year before. For the two of them everything had changed dramatically. Mouse had since dated a dancer from the school and had hung out with many of the students on various occasions. Tupac had become a genuine veteran of the school. Comfortably they ran about the once strange ballroom and hallways, wreaking as much havoc as possible, following girls into bathrooms, and teasing some of the more humorous masqueraders.

After everyone had had a chance to mill about and enjoy the party, we again made the move downstairs into the hallway by the cafeteria, this time to kick off round two. But from the very beginning it was not at all the same. No one was focused on the event. The energy and hype, pomp and ceremony of the previous year's showdown was simply not there. The crowd of people was much smaller as many had left the ball early that year, and the vibe in the air was more one of a friendly game than an adversarial showdown.

Jada and Linda set it off by rockin' "You're a Hot Bitch." Actually, I wouldn't say they "rocked" it. They sounded good, but not at all the way I had coached them, how I had envisioned the rhyme being performed when writing it. But it was cool; they added their own flavor to it. Instead of reciting the rhyme in its entirety, finishing all of the verses, they cut it short at a point in the middle, sending the focus back to Joyce and her crew in the back and forth, "quick hit" manner in which we usually flowed in The Dozens. They basically carried the duel like another of the daily sessions rather than a formal, prime-time exhibition. Joyce and her friends replied in kind, also sounding good but not noticeably better in any real way. Each of the crews spiced up their lyrical endeavors with little choreographed dances, giving the "rap battle" more of a sorority showdown feel. It was a very different affair.

As soon as the girls finished, Tupac, still clad in his award-winning attire, as if ushering them off, stepped into the focus of those few still around and recited a rhyme with Mouse backing him up on the beatbox. But the excitement was simply not there. The small crowd had already dispersed. It was over and no one had won or lost. Instead of staying at the ball like we did the previous year, everyone went over to John's, where he and Tupac hosted an after party that lasted into the morning.

At John's house, Tupac was able to enjoy a very different life than what he was used to. John's room was a large loft area overlooking the living room, with plenty of space, and plenty of the comforts of upper middle-class living. And John generously shared with his needy friend. This generosity Tupac accepted without guilt or feeling at all out of line. Tupac would wear various articles of John's clothing as if they were his own. He wasn't particular or anal about what he wore, or its condition: clean, previously worn, whatever. I remember him, on several occasions, wearing an item of clothing that John had just worn the day before. Even previously worn, just one day removed, John's shirts and pants were nicer than Tupac's own stuff.

John was not alone in providing this sort of support to the popular School for the Arts personality. Many of Tupac's classmates would give him clothes to wear: either flatly donated or purchased as a Christmas, birthday, or some other kind of gift. In particular I remember him receiving a lot of clothes at Christmas. One day near the Christmas holiday of that year Tupac walked into the cafeteria with a whole bunch of gift boxes that had been ripped open and reassembled. There was torn wrapping paper dangling from them and various pieces of clothing poking through the tops. Accounting for much of this gift giving was the throng of white girls around the school that seemed to be enthralled with Tupac; they couldn't get enough *Tupac*. They saw these gifts as an opportunity to get close, wanting to in some way be associated with him, even jumping at the opportunity to go out and buy him something he genuinely needed.

What a different reality this all was from that which he would have experienced at a normal high school. It was a good thing he had been accepted into the unique school for more reasons than one. Besides the creative curriculum which provided breathing space for dynamic personalities such as his, the extremely lax standards and expectations with regard to dress relieved a great deal of pressure from students such as him and myself who couldn't afford any of the latest fashions.

Mouse also has memories of Tupac's time over at John's. Looking back, he sees them as profoundly influential. This surrogate world of his friend's was strange and entirely new, a kind of parallel universe, thriving and free, yet nonexistent to the one he had known his entire life. It was like the sixties in eighties clothing.

Everyone was all about partying with no inhibition permitted. The girls were fine and the guys behaved as if testosterone was something to be neutralized and hidden. Everyone beamed the smile of plenty; no one had an attitude. The beer and herb would be flowing, the music hanging out in the background, people becoming more and more loose with every hour. Since he didn't smoke (or drink very much) Mouse would simply pretend to be high, like everyone else, exuding a certain airiness and lightness of temperament in order to join in on the love fest. How different it all was from Greenmount and Old York Road.

Soon John would move out of his parents' house and into his older brother's apartment in Reservoir Hill, less than a mile away: a nice neighborhood yet much more in the mix of the city's poorer areas. When he made this move, he left the way open for Tupac to come with him, an offer Tupac immediately accepted. Having grown used to his newfound comfort and freedom, Tupac had no intention of returning to his old life in his old neighborhood at his mother's apartment, and thanks to John, he didn't have to.

Tupac took up little space at the two-bedroom apartment. He and John slept on separate couches in the living room while John's brother and a friend of his named Richard took the two bedrooms. It was at this time that I began to hang out with the two of them a lot more, the innocent, naïve addition to this quietly infamous crew of well-experienced bad boys. John was a quiet guy who, like Tupac, was in the midst of a lot of drama in his life related to both family and school. They were both rebellious spirits who enjoyed looking at things differently from everyone else, living as fully as humanly possible, and contemplating, deeply, all that was around them. Without fear or sloth they would explore this liveliness, this contemplation, employing the full weight of their popularity. Stoically, they would undertake expeditions through deeper thoughts and meaning, dissecting and discussing all they found to be intriguing, alluring, looking for all sorts of interesting clues in unlikely places, from sorcery to communism. They were always reading about this stuff, from a fascinating array of obscure titles and authors. And in marathon discussions (often chemically fueled and inspired) they would deal with the same, a favorite topic being the esoteric, the metaphysical. Sometimes when they would embark on one of these discussions, my eyes would glaze over as my mind would retreat and return to a more familiar place. But they would feed off each other and keep going and going, deeper.

The two boys' mutual acquaintance with Jada facilitated their rapidly developing friendship. And they remained friends after John and Jada broke up. I entered the circle through my friendship with Tupac. I had known John for over three years at the school, but never would have thought to befriend him outside of school. We had nothing in common as far as I was concerned; the same way I felt about the white kids in the school in general. They were doing their thing, and I was doing mine. We neither knew nor understood each other, with no real desire to. What for? But Tupac saw things differently. He *was* interested in John and the white crowd in school. And he went about fostering those friendships from day one.

Tupac got along well with the white students. Around them he was able to exist without the usual hang-ups, to explore sides of himself that he had to keep buried and quiet otherwise. But in this environment, as well, he could not simply be himself. I always sensed a feeling of work when I observed him around the white students. It seemed he always had to show that he was intelligent, that he wasn't some "ignorant nigga." Sometimes it seemed like he was overdoing it. I observed how he was around Mouse and Gerard and other Black kids, and then how he was around John and the white kids, and there was a definite difference. I then began to wonder if he felt he had to just respond differently to certain people. I would ask myself, "Is this what I have to do to be friends with these folks? Should I be this way as well? Should I act this way and talk this way around John and them?" But I couldn't do it. I refused to do it. Having been financially unable to conform around my neighborhood and in school for so many years, and growing used to living that way, with well-developed defenses and a deeply engrained bitterness toward all who might make me feel uncomfortable, I had no desire to conform to anything that did not come naturally, either Black or white. So this represented way too far a stretch for me. But it wasn't too far a stretch for Tupac. Though he lightly contorted himself at times, he was always in control. He knew they needed him. He understood what it meant to be the lone Black friend (or one of few) to many of these kids, to be their connection to a Black world that was taking over the airwaves (both TV and radio) and that had been the majority in Baltimore for many years. He didn't mind playing the role, being the connection. There were many benefits. Most importantly, he was fucking all the girls.

For the first time I peeked into this other world that had been all around me ever since ninth grade. Following Tupac's lead I saw things I had never seen before, and did things I had never done. My life was opening up.

John was bussing tables at a prestigious restaurant down near the Inner Harbor where he was able to get jobs for me and Tupac, and later Mouse. As a result of our increased association through work, I began to spend more time at their apartment. We had a lot of good times over there, playing records, talking shit, writing rhymes. A favorite pastime of theirs was smoking herb. I wasn't down with it and they respected that, never once attempting to pressure me into it. Whenever they smoked they would go into one of the bedrooms, leaving me out in the living room to chill by myself until their return. But on one particular day when I was feeling the compounded effect of an array of stresses in my life, soon after their ritual journey into the bedroom, I followed, feeling both curious and particularly rebellious. By the time I entered the room they had turned off the regular lights and were seated, instead, under the soft glow of a single red light, creating a sort of mystical atmosphere in the room. John handed me the joint to take a hit and Tupac looked at him as if to say, "What are you doing?" After I took a few hits I started to cough and passed it to Tupac. That was it. I started to get silly and didn't stop. I started rapping and couldn't shut up, turning everything into a rap. Tupac repeatedly told me to shut up and I simply replied with a rap about him telling me to shut up. At first it was funny but it became extremely annoying, especially to Tupac, who would get mellow when he smoked. After a while he left the room and I eventually rapped myself to sleep. The next morning I felt as if someone had hit me in the head with a brick. Tupac and John were also sluggish and we all woke up a little late; we had smoked a lot. We joked about the previous night. John found it funny, but Tupac talked about never giving me another joint, ever again. All in all I liked the experience. I liked the invigorating feeling of doing something spontaneous, something against what I had always simply accepted as true because that's what I had been told all my life; it was liberating. My first time smoking was with Tupac Shakur. Somehow I even thought of it as such back then.

My presence in the smoke session that evening definitely put a twist on the normal vibe. They would always get "deep" in their talking after returning from a smoke session, often ending up on the philosophies and lessons of Charles Thompson, a distinguished local spiritualist to whom they had been introduced by Jada's aunt. Had I not disrupted their usual flow, Charles Thompson would have likely been one of the topics of discussion in a more mellow and thoughtful affair. Mr. Thompson's teachings dealt with sorcery and the metaphysical, with higher levels of thought: their favorite. Tupac and John shared a great deal in their lives during this period. In many ways Tupac looked up to John, studying him as I studied Tupac. John represented a kind of big brother figure to him, providing him with instruction through example on facets of life and society with which Tupac was unversed and unfamiliar. But a turn would come about in their relationship that would leave Tupac very disoriented.

Birth of
Born Busy

Tupac and Mouse entered yet another citywide talent contest in which they thought they would certainly take first place. There was really no reason for them to enter more contests. They *always* won. Losing (finishing lower than first place) was simply not even a possibility to Tupac; the concept did not exist. With more than enough ego for several highly confident people, he had proclaimed for some time that if he ever lost a battle, any battle, whether it be against some cat in the street or in the formal setting of a contest, he would retire from the pursuit altogether, because there was no second place; either you were the best or you were nothing. But lose is exactly what he and Mouse did, as far as Tupac was concerned.

The contest was held at the main branch of the Enoch Pratt Free Library in downtown Baltimore where they had begun their contest career, unblemished until this day of their return over three years later. This time they performed their "Babies Having Babies" rap, a banner piece of theirs used in several of the city-sponsored, adult-judged contests: not only for its attractively positive message, but also its mild use of words. A strategic-thinking emerging artist, serious about success, always gives careful consideration to his audience. But this time the plan did not work. This time they came in second place, a completely unacceptable outcome, and they were pissed. Never before had they been second best. And making matters worse (or better, depending on one's perspective) they were defeated by a group of little girls who had won on no more than the merit of their age and cuteness. Tupac refused to accept this defeat, feeling that the political influences behind the so-called loss were obvious. As far as he and Mouse were concerned, they were the true winners. And everyone in the audience agreed. Many of them made sure to tell the boys as much after the contest. But still, the loss was taken deeply to heart; they were hurt, badly. Without flinching Tupac told of the "loss" upon his return to school and immediately honored his oath. He said he had retired from rap and would never return.

At first I thought he was just unduly dramatic about the whole thing. He had a way of being overly dramatic when faced with some thing or situation he didn't like. But then I thought about it, and realized the attention he would get by not rapping. I sensed strategy in the move.

Tupac ran this bit with every semblance of sincerity for quite a while. People would try their best to talk him out of it, pumping him up, trying to lure him into bustin' out just one rhyme; but he would not budge. He maintained his record had been tarnished beyond repair. But there was an unspoken agenda very different from what he was telling all of the anxiously listening, concerned ears around him. Like that, he went from rapper extraordinaire to promoter extraordinaire. He saw that everyone was beginning to take him for granted. And he saw the perfect opportunity to do something about it.

Tupac was one of the stars of the school and kids wanted to hear from him. They wanted to hear their king of rap do his thing: just what he'd wanted, and even engineered. The painful aftermath of the loss was effectively transformed into a contrived break from the scene, after which, at the right time (and not a second sooner), he would come back fresh, making another grand entrance, showcasing all of his new rhymes and flows developed in secret during his time away.

Tupac had a habit of doing things as theater, just to get a reaction, and to bring attention to himself. And when doing so, he liked to test the waters, exploring exactly how far he could go, and how many he could get to follow. He was well aware of his popularity.

One day I saw him in the basement hall by the cafeteria wearing only shorts. He was coming from the pool. Since we had no gymnasium, and no gym period, students often swam for exercise and recreation either on breaks between classes or at lunch. I noticed him smiling as he walked up to me. The force of his smile made me smile as well. I could tell something was up.

"Yo, Herb just touched my chest, and was like, 'Wow,' " he said, smiling, lightly pushing his index finger into his pectoral muscle. And then, pointing to his stomach, ". . . touched my stomach like, 'Wow.' " He was very amused by this. We laughed but the vision I had in my mind of Herb actually doing this disgusted me. How could anyone bite so hard?

Tupac often played on the fact that other kids admired him; his ego had a way of running wild. He would do such off the wall things as paint his fingernails black, and walk around school all day with a pink baby bottle at which he would suckle nonstop, like some kind of pacifier. Other times he would wear eyeliner. When I first saw someone else, a white kid in his class, do the same, I just laughed to myself. He was all up in people's heads.

And Tupac could always be found in class or strutting through the halls shirtless with his vain, skinny ass. As a theater student he had the excuse of productions and rehearsals, which provided all the green light he needed. Of course the more risqué of these experiments he began after moving in with John. He was already a marked man in his own neighborhood and could by no means return home in such a way. But around the school and nonthreatening environment of the surrounding areas, including John's neighborhood, he was free to do as he wished. Having found an environment in which he could run as wild as he liked, he took full advantage.

Now more than a year removed from the initial battle, "*The* Battle," I had long since gotten smart and quickly decided that if I couldn't beat'm, I was going to join'm. And I did. Tupac had become a close friend, even crew. However, Gerard was still my main man; the two of us represented a crew in and of ourselves. We had been extremely close ever since our second year at the school over two years before and had grown to be quite serious about our music making. Gerard was an excellent DJ, adept at finding and creating good beats. I spent many hours at his house, in his little bedroom, writing and performing rhymes to the various beats he would sample and develop. A lot of these hours stretched late into the night, with his neighbor banging on the wall to signal to us to quiet down. This became an expected part of our routine. Whenever there were no knocks on the wall we were thrown off, and would turn up the music to see if we could return to a more familiar place. Sure enough, the knocking would follow soon afterward. We made a game out of it.

Gerard got all of his equipment from his father, who was an electronics and stereo system buff. Upgrading his system regularly, Gerard's father would pass down to his son all of his old stuff. And Gerard learned to master this equipment, and with it made some pretty impressive music. Sometimes I would stay over his house for days on end, to the point that Mr. and Mrs. Young all but adopted me as their own.

However, as Tupac and I began to hang together more, this routine changed, and my time over at Gerard's decreased considerably. We began to coordinate more and more with regard to rhyming, writing new songs together, and practicing tirelessly. Hearing Tupac flow, I knew he would add a whole new dimension to the sessions over at Gerard's. It was time to bring the two worlds together. I hooked it up with Gerard, and Tupac and I went over to his house together.

It was on a Saturday afternoon sometime in the middle of the second semester of that year. We took the bus over to Gerard's house, which was only seven or eight blocks from Tupac's mother's apartment. But those seven or eight blocks represented a huge difference in neighborhoods. Gerard's house was in a middle-class Black neighborhood of single-family homes on a small side street off of Greenmount Avenue. His parents were both professional people, and the house looked the part: a toned down version of Cosby utopia. Entering the house we marched right up to his room and settled in. Gerard immediately walked over to his turntables and began to feel out the beat from LL Cool J's "I Need A Beat" (the instrumental version). Tupac took the mic casually, as if to test it out, but instead launched a full-fledged rap without one bell or whistle excluded for expediency. Through to the last line, he pressed forward, salivating at the opportunity and knowing no less than one hundred percent effort. To deny my marveling at the sight, the sheer efficiency and spontaneous fluidity, would be untrue. Needing no time to acclimate himself, he flipped the switch, opened his heart, and poured it out before us without hesitation. Afterward we fooled around a little more, listening to more beats and freestyling rhymes. It was a good session.

The following day at school Gerard pulled out a little box and played a tape for me that he had made of Tupac's piece from the previous night. I just smiled. I knew how pumped Tupac would be. We took it with us to lunch. When we played it for him in the cafeteria he beamed widely for a few moments, listening closely. He then went busily about shepherding in anyone who walked by to hear him on tape. It didn't matter who it was, people he had never spoken to before, whoever. It was one of the first times he had ever heard himself recorded. After another session over at Gerard's we decided to form a group. For several days we all went about thinking of possible names for our new crew and then I came up with "Born Busy." I was particularly happy with the invention and knew that everyone would agree. Our next session together we all agreed, and it became official. We were Born Busy.

On His Own:
First Apartment

Tupac was terribly confused and upset by what transpired between him and John. When he arrived home to the Reservoir Hill apartment one day a couple of months into the second semester of the school year, he found John and a friend of John's named Jonathan sitting in the living room laughing and joking around. He joined the conversation, when all of a sudden John announced that he would have to find another place to live. John then went on to explain that his brother was moving to another apartment building in which he had landed a new job as manager, and that he and Jonathan were moving in with him, but there was no room for Tupac. Tupac was shocked by the coldness and insensitivity of the announcement; apparently John had even laughed as he made it.

This stunned Tupac. He felt betrayed, that John had easily disregarded their close friendship developed through so many hours together, so many heart-to-heart conversations and experiences. John felt that Tupac just wanted him as a crutch. And he didn't want to be that crutch any longer. But Tupac's life had grown so intertwined with John's that he hadn't any short-term plan that did not include John's pivotal presence, and all it had provided. He had nowhere to go. Returning to his mother's was out of the question, as it would mean doing so in defeat, to the same imbalance and struggle that he had left in the first place. This was a difficult time for him. There were hard decisions to make. He grew up very quickly. Throughout this period, Tupac wrote John a number of heartfelt letters telling him how he felt about the whole situation. John felt that Tupac was being overdramatic, as he had a tendency to do when he didn't like something. He felt Tupac was just trying to manipulate him, and so he continued to keep his distance.

When the move was complete and John and his brother had gone, Tupac ended up staying on in the apartment with Richard, John's brother's friend and original roommate. The two were a very unlikely couple. Richard was a short, slender, older white guy in his late twenties with shortly cropped brown hair, an assortment of business suits, and an apparently lucrative job in sales: a yuppie. Somehow Tupac convinced Richard of his ability and resolve to produce, every month, half of the rent for the large two-bedroom apartment. More accurately, Richard simply hadn't the heart to throw him out. Still, the two of them got along surprisingly well . . . that is until the rent was due.

Tupac searched for acting jobs and landed a commercial for WJZ-TV channel 13, the local ABC affiliate. The commercial was a news promotion, for which he was likely never to receive any pay in the first place. But Tupac sincerely believed otherwise, if only because he had so thoroughly convinced himself, and waited faithfully for a check. Regularly, he would burst out in anger and disappointment directed toward the leisurely and later fraudulent (in his adamant opinion) television station. The check was supposed to be for three hundred and fifty dollars; amazing, considering this was the exact amount he owed for the rent. "Is it really three hundred fifty dollars?" I asked when we were alone, not willing to believe the unlikely coincidence, especially after seeing the commercial. You couldn't even see his face, just the back of his head in a crowd of other students. But he stuck to his story.

We were still bussing tables. However, the little we made was far from sufficient. Tupac was back and forth to his mother's apartment throughout this period. She called often, to check on him, and regularly sent food. I almost lived at the apartment myself. Whatever money we had, primarily from working at the restaurant, we shared with each other. And whenever I could bring food I did. Sometimes I would bring big warehouse-sized boxes of Oodles of Noodles from my grandmother's, and they would disappear in no time. I learned to not expect any to be left when I came back around to the apartment after being away for more than a day. Tupac liked his Oodles of Noodles real soupy, with two flavor packs in each batch, and extra water. The noodles from the second pack he simply discarded, like the product was supposed to be prepared that way. At first I hated this perversion of the familiar food item, but I started to get used to it. We would cut up whatever was in the fridge, throw it all in the pot, and make a meal of it: from hotdogs to broccoli, carrots and other vegetables, and all kinds of condiments, it didn't matter. Oodles of Noodles was a familiar staple for Tupac.

We spent so much time together over at Tupac's apartment that it became a source of friction within my family. I was staying over there for even longer stints than I had at Gerard's. We were at the age where we wanted to do as we wished. We felt we had what it took, that we were smart enough and sufficiently capable of governing our own lives. And we told our respective mothers (in my case, my grandmother whom I called "Ma") as much.

In this time together at the apartment we became very comfortable with each other. In fact, we had quietly become family. The similarity of our financial situations and artistic understanding provided for us a common ground. Erasing the question mark of each new day and each hour was our most binding common attribute, our strong ambition. We wanted to be the best, and were willing to work for it. Hour after hour we spent pursuing our passion, never once wasting even a second with questions of feasibility. We would sit in that apartment all day long, dreaming of amazing alternate realities, writing rhymes, rehearsing, or just listening to music, floating off into our own little worlds. The old brownstone apartment had hardwood floors, old furniture, and impressionistic shadows which hung lazily beyond the ambient daylight which trickled in from the large bay windows in the front. Tupac would be seated on the couch facing into the apartment, smoking cigarette after cigarette. I would watch the curling smoke rise upward from the burning ember held delicately between index and middle fingers at a slant from his closely cropped head. His thumb would be pressed into his temple as he looked down to the notepad, writing out lyrics on the wooden coffee table in the center of the room in front of him. This common posture always made me envision smoky pictures of Miles Davis writing out sheet music under lamplight in a dark room. I would view the scene from the chair on the other side of the room (John and his brother having taken the other couch with them when they left), deeper into the interior of the apartment, facing out, also writing out lyrics on a notepad, pausing regularly to recite them quietly to myself before continuing.

Looking at him during these times I was always struck by the irony of the intense peacefulness, the quiet, even though it was now something I had seen on countless occasions. It just seemed so out of place in some way. Not merely because the disposition seemed awkward and a bit unnatural on the often loud, boisterous young boy, but because it would seem so on any boy his age, or mine. There was a deep-seated maturity about this adolescent that suggested years well beyond his own. I would catch him unconsciously poring his gaze over some random object as he grabbed with equal unconsciousness the fat of his upper lip, repeatedly, pulling on it lightly between index finger and thumb, and releasing it to return to its original position where it would quiver in place, the pen almost forgotten in his other hand. Many hours I saw him pass in this manner. There was a colossal problem out there, almost insurmountable in its difficulty, and he was figuring it out: computing.

 **Bedroom Studio**

It was in this same period, late second semester of Tupac's junior and my senior year, that we began to meet regularly at Gerard's to record the rhymes that Tupac and I had been writing at his apartment. After hearing himself on tape following our initial session up in Gerard's bedroom, Tupac was hooked. He immediately felt comfortable with Gerard, and with the idea of the three of us working together. Born Busy was formed, and the bedroom was made our official studio.

At Gerard's house Tupac added an interesting contrasting presence to the sterile, etiquette-driven existence presided over by Gerard's straitlaced parents. He had known little restraint in his life and possessed no concept of much of what most of us consider basic understanding with regard to general societal protocol. For example, when at the center of a casual conversation inclusive of Gerard's mother, a friend of hers, and several other guests at Gerard's graduation cookout, Tupac, without thinking, voiced a candid judgment of the problem between two obviously feuding teens. He bluntly suggested their problem was the result of their recently having sex and their inability to deal with the accompanying difficulty and complexity. Gerard and I tried signaling to him to cut it short, but this just drove him to further detail his analysis, double-checking every word within to reaffirm that there was nothing in need of censor.

"What?!" he demanded when my head dropped with disgust and my hands came down loudly against my thighs. "You don't say this stuff around people's parents, man," I said, shaking my head, as upset with him as I was embarrassed. All I could think was, "Please don't say anything about smoking herb!"

"What?!" he just repeated, now a little angry himself.

"Just keep on talking, Tupac," Mrs. Young interjected with a smile. "What's wrong? He's just talking." She found the whole thing amusing, and continued to egg him on in order to get as much out of him as she could. After that Tupac was one of her favorites. Anytime I walked through their door alone, she would inevitably ask for Tupac. But because of my comments, he started distrusting the environment. Soon after his comments I pulled him aside and tried to make him understand how the things he was saying were inappropriate. This perplexed him. Out of nowhere, as we walked out of the house after the cookout, he said that he never wanted to be over there unless I was there to make sure he didn't say anything too off the wall.

This subtle friction that Tupac felt at Gerard's house had no effect on our development as a group. Tupac and I continued to go over to Gerard's and rehearse and record. One morning Tupac and I planned to meet at Gerard's as usual. I told him I was heading over there and he said he would be over later. Gerard and I fooled around with some tracks and talked about various things in preparation for the session. After a couple hours passed, we just started to do whatever, hanging out like we used to, waiting for Tupac to show up. By the time he arrived, it was evening and Jada was with him. The two of them were all smiles. Gerard and I were pissed.

Tupac led the way up into the room, all enthusiastic, immediately going about touching and messing with all of the equipment. He got on the turntables and pretended to scratch and mix, showing off for Jada like he had been working the equipment all along. "Yo, play that thing for Jada," he told Gerard, talking about the tape of him reciting "When Will You Learn" at the very first session. "Where y'all comin' from?" I asked, as if he should have known to volunteer that information from the beginning. "Yo, we got a videotape," he replied, pulling a black tape from his pants pocket. He was wearing another of his select few uniforms, a black tank top with black stretch pants, thus the unusually large capacity of his pants pockets.

We went down into the basement and Gerard popped in the tape; it was of Tupac and Jada at King's Dominion Amusement Park performing a DJ Jazzy Jeff and the Fresh Prince song. "Y'all was at King's Dominion?" was our immediate question. We were really pissed then. We had been in the studio all day, waiting for him, putting things together for the group, and he was out having a ball at King's Dominion. And then he had the nerve to sit there and flaunt the proof. I couldn't believe it. Not only did he leave us hanging when we were expecting him, but they didn't even bother to invite me and Gerard along for the day of fun at King's Dominion. When I later asked him about it, he said that Jada called him out of the blue when she and her family were about to leave, and he wanted to go, so he went. But I'm pretty sure they knew about it the day before. I was highly pissed, but I let it go. We went back up into the bedroom and had a casual session. Jada hung out with us for the rest of the night.

Tupac and Mouse had been somewhat estranged over the course of the year, stemming from Mouse's absence from the after school fight the previous spring. But as time tempered his animosity, Tupac began to speak of Mouse, and we considered all that Mouse would contribute to the group if he were made a member. Not long after the cookout, Tupac brought Mouse by Gerard's for one of our music sessions. The feeling was less than comfortable at first. Tupac and I kicked off the session with two rhymes that we had written together, "Check it Out," and "That's My Man Throwin' Down," reciting them a cappella into the tape recorder mic. This was the first time Mouse had seen Tupac and me rhyme together, the first time he had seen anyone else rhyme with Tupac the way they had from the age of thirteen up until that year. I could tell he was a little uncomfortable.

He and Tupac went next. They hit a couple of their rhymes. By the end of the session all uneasiness was completely burned off and forgotten. We talked a lot, joked around, and hit rhymes off and on: some previously composed, some freestyle. Mouse and Gerard even engaged in a beat battle: Mouse on the mic, and Gerard on the turntable. And we taped everything. Before we knew it, it was late. But still we continued for as long as we could, lowering our voices and the volume of the music, continuing through the tell-tale banging on the wall from the neighbors. Gerard would hold on to the tape from this session and present it to me more than eight years later. The four of us definitely had something, and we all felt it.

The Twenty-Man Battle

Often after work, before going home, we would walk around the corner to "The Block," a seedy stretch of Baltimore Street in the middle of downtown full of sex shops and strip joints, where we would grab a bite to eat and play video games at an all-night greasy spoon spot called Crazy John's. If not at Crazy John's we could be found over at Hopkins Plaza, just past the Inner Harbor, rehearsing our rhymes on the large permanent stage there. School was out for the summer, so we hung out at will. It would be around one o'clock in the morning when we would take over the plaza, when it was completely deserted and we could make as much noise as we wanted, practicing what Tupac called our "stage presence" without interruption.

On one such evening, after a long and busy shift, we busted through the double front doors of the lobby below the restaurant and out into the warm, moist summer air wafting in off the bay. The humidity was noticeable (never is it not in the summer in Baltimore) but not overbearing. Casually we walked down the small, dark, alleylike street alongside the restaurant in the opposite direction of the harbor. The buildings rising tall to each side of us refused all but trace parcels of the bright light sent forth into the evening darkness of downtown from the brilliantly lit buildings of Harbor Place. We took our time walking through The Block, peeking past obnoxious, burly characters and curtains meant to obstruct the otherwise perfect view of naked ladies dancing on bars and walking about. We did not stop at Crazy John's. With two new additions to our repertoire of raps yet to be ironed out, we were eager to rehearse.

When we arrived at the familiar square it was wide open and deserted as usual. The deep, thick shadows all around were held at bay by small, sparsely placed lamps dimly lighting the inner region of the oversize square and its huge stage. With the familiarity of home we hopped up onto the stage, murmuring a few random lines under our breath, making accompanying bodily gestures just to get the blood flowing. Then we collected ourselves and began. As usual, Tupac had the first verse. He kicked off the session with "We Work Hard," his favorite of all the songs we had written: "We work hard to give you rhymes that put the groove in your butts / To make your body shake and shiver to the razor sharp cuts / It's not an easy thing to do if you're a rapper you know / I swear to God it's so hard to make the crowd go ho! / But yo I am persistent and I won't stop until the perpetrators drop, and my crew's on top / Sometimes I wanna give up, but I persist / And if you think it's all easy then listen to this / We work hard!" During his verses I would jump in at certain points to emphasize certain words. And he would do the same in mine. At these points we would use visuals as well, to drive the meaning home. Like on "hard!" in the line "We work hard!" we would both point to flexed biceps, consciously continuing to move around the stage. We called this "working the stage."

Tupac always wrote his verses with only a bare minimum of words for me to interject. Yet he always wanted to say a bunch of words in my verses. And his style was such that I couldn't jump in on his verses uninvited, like he did in mine when I tried to give him a taste of his own medicine and included only a bare minimum of words for him to contribute. He would push his way into my verses, and barrel forward through his own, changing speeds and drawing out words. I guess he had to be in charge. And in many ways he was. I pretty much gave him that, at least with respect to talent. There was no delusion in my mind of our being equal talents as far as rapping was concerned. He was without doubt the anchorman of the group. But I definitely saw us as equal members with regard to the activities, plans, and general decision-making of the group. And I always made sure to produce just as much work as he, and to at least hold my own with respect to the quality of my rhymes and flow.

After a couple of iterations of the new song, we were nailing the lyrics comfortably, and began to further explore the more physical attributes of the holistic presentation, our stage presence. We were on the second song when out of the darkness a large group of guys appeared heading directly toward us; it was approaching one o'clock in the morning.

"Darrin, I sense some trouble . . . that's a lotta guys; let's go," Tupac said, ready to make a break for it. I sensed the same, but they had already taken note of us, and running would have only baited them instinctively into the hunt. So I said no, and recommended we continue rehearsing as if we didn't see them. Dressed in our "penguin suits," bus boy uniforms of thrift store quality, thin black slacks, equally cheap white dress shirts discolored with food stains, and black dress shoes, we must have appeared as ideal targets. Glancing up to sneak a look, I saw a couple of the guys openly carrying guns in their hands, and some had blood splattered all over their shirts. When they got a little closer we could hear them talking about how they had just beaten up some guy down at Harbor Place. We just kept rocking our rhymes and working the stage back and forth, acting, as much as possible, as if we didn't even notice them. They continued to approach and finally came up to the stage, standing at the edge and looking up at us. I recognized one of the guys from middle school. He recognized me as well and spoke. We were saved! They may have been a bit thrown by our nonchalant disposition, but this may very well have been what saved our asses because they were definitely on the prowl.

All twenty guys then jumped on the stage, asking us daringly, with huffs and puffs, if we thought we were good. Tupac replied with equal cockiness, asking them if they wanted to battle.

"Fuck, yeah!" at least half of them replied at once, the gun toters retiring their weapons to their waistbands. The whole crew became visibly pumped up. . . . It was on. Just Tupac and myself against twenty guys. We went first and they followed, teaming up on us two at a time. Tupac and I rocked every rhyme we had written, making no mistakes. All of the many hours of rehearsal paid off beautifully. We went through all twenty of them. And after they ran out of rhymes, we rocked the two we had just practiced, just to knock them completely out the box. It was obvious that we had won, but instead of bowing in defeat they then wanted to dance against us.

Although break dancing was all but forgotten by then, dancing in general was as big as ever with the emergence of countless popular dances on the hip-hop and club music scenes. So we obliged them and handed them their second defeat. In this portion of the battle I took the lead and saw to it that the victory was ours. Tupac was notoriously left-footed on both legs. And his contribution was less than impressive. I, on the other hand, had had plenty experience with the popular dances of the time since I frequented a big under-aged club near the harbor where I regularly danced against whole crews of guys. I pulled out everything I knew that night, and even made up new stuff on the fly.

At this the intimidating gang surrendered in defeat, smacking our hands and giving us our respect. Generously, they offered compliments and asked us if we wanted to hang with them. Tupac and I looked to each other, smiling, and then back to them: "Cool." So we headed off with them down Baltimore Street. We must have looked pretty odd, the two of us in our bus boy uniforms, roaming the streets with this blood-splattered army of Murphy Homes (probably the most notorious housing project in Baltimore) ruffians. We ended up at Crazy John's, buying food and playing video games. "You know we beat'm right?" Tupac said to me quietly. All I could think was, don't say that too loud.

At Crazy John's, Tupac entered a zone, playing games with new zeal, like it was something he did all the time, like he was actually attempting to break into the high scores; but I knew differently. He was little more of a video game person than I; and I wasn't much of one at all. This went on for what seemed like an eternity: just talking, playing games, buying pizza—in short, spending all of our hard-earned tips. Tupac was still nowhere near full of the experience when I noticed the time approaching three o'clock in the morning. I was exhausted, and tired of hanging with these dudes and spending all of my money, but Tupac wanted to hang longer. Out of earshot from everyone else, I told him that I was ready to leave. He strongly resisted a couple of times, debating the issue, but after I told him that I would leave him there, he finally agreed and we bid our good-byes to the crew. They told us that they hung out there at Crazy John's a lot if we ever wanted to hook up with them again. We clasped hands and hugged the guys nearest to us and walked out.

This was obviously a meaningful experience for Tupac, judging from the way he vibed through the whole affair and fought so hard to keep it going regardless of the time. We had worked all night long, and I, for one, was worn out. But Tupac was ready to keep going, like a kid on Christmas morning. It felt good to him to be appreciated by cats on the street, the same type of kids that had given him so much grief since his arrival in Baltimore, and probably in New York as well. They had made no issue of his clothing. Despite our ridiculous appearance, we were in work uniforms and therefore free of the normal scrutiny of gear that was both of our undying nemesis beyond the walls of the school. And for Tupac, this curse was generally much more menacing due to that X-factor about him that always seemed to bring out the worst in already "bad" people. But these kids did not buck on us, as he was used to. They took us in with open arms, knowing no more about us than the dope-ass rhymes we just kicked.

We walked out of Crazy John's bolstered and triumphant, with an extra spring to our step as we embarked on the journey uptown to Tupac's apartment, several miles away. At the corner of Howard and Monument Streets, still downtown, we came upon the Little X theater. Tupac pointed without expression: "Let's check this shit out," he said, equally void of expression, before walking right in the door. I followed behind him. I had never been there before, but Tupac knew exactly where he was going. Without looking around, he walked up to the ticket counter and we purchased our tickets. They were surprisingly cheap, less than a dollar apiece. As we walked in the theater I was immediately struck by the focus of the camera shot on the large screen. There was no movie scene before us, as I expected, with characters and some form of setting, only a huge penis ramming into a huge ass, spanning the entire surface area of the screen, and loud shouts and smacking sounds coming from speakers somewhere in the darkness. There were only six or seven people spaced sparsely throughout. I noticed a noise to my left and discovered a guy jerking off feverishly in one of the back seats when I looked over. Tupac also noticed the guy, and commented loud enough for everyone to hear as we continued down the aisle, "Damn, mawfuckas in here jerkin' off and shit!" It was pretty nasty in there. The floor was sticky and there was litter all over a lot of the seats. We stayed in there for about a half an hour before leaving in silence.

The entire walk home, there was just silence, not a single word. I knew he was thinking the same thing I was, "Damn, I want some ass!" Back then, at that age, it was a little harder to "go all the way" than it is for older guys. So I started scanning through all the various girls I knew, thinking, "Aright, who I gotta sweat for like three weeks to get some ass?"

When we turned from Park Avenue onto Lenox Street, we saw that Richard's red pickup was not parked in front of the apartment building, which meant he wasn't home. He was always away from home, whether with his girlfriend, or otherwise absent from the apartment. That was all the better for us, since we could monopolize the place with impunity. We stepped into the apartment and I plopped down on the sofa in the living room. "Yeah, man, I'm going to bed," Tupac said, finally breaking the silence. Then with that same blank look I had seen so many times, "Yeah, man, you take the couch. . . . You need a blanket?" he said, heading over to the table against the wall by Richard's room. From the table he grabbed a magazine and headed back toward me. Leaning over the coffee table, he picked up his pack of cigarettes, and folded what I then saw was a porno magazine under his arm.

"Yo, I'm uh smoke a cigarette, look at my magazine, and me and my hand . . ." he said dryly, looking at his right hand held up at eye level, fingers in the shape of a mitten. He turned and began toward his room. "Me and my hand," he calmly repeated several times while walking, the magazine under his left arm, cigarettes in his left hand, the whole way looking at the raised hand. "And I'm uh call it a night," he finished at his door. "Yo . . . good night yo," he said before going in the room and closing the door.

To Be a Shakespearean Actor

Although rap was Tupac's true love, the variety of music he listened to was amazing. This became clear to me one Saturday morning when he, Richard, and I sat around the living room of the apartment in our boxer shorts and undershirts talking about music. Richard was definitely a cool guy, who had a pleasant disposition and a free-flowing approach to life. His bedroom door was never closed, even when his girlfriend was in there with him. In the mornings I would see them lying on his single mattress on the floor (no box spring underneath), still asleep. I showed him respect, and he was always cool to me. No matter how much time I spent there at the apartment, he never gave me even the slightest hint of a bad vibe. We periodically had chill sessions when he was around (which wasn't a whole lot). And when I wasn't there, he and Tupac would bond.

In this Saturday morning discussion, Tupac floated along with Richard easily, unmoved by any of his older roommate's detours in various directions that were completely unfamiliar to me. Despite Richard's dramatically different background and social orientation, Tupac never once lost his footing, and comfortably expounded upon many of the different artists who came up over the course of the conversation which spanned the full spectrum. From LL Cool J to Peter Gabriel, and Sun Ra and Jimi Hendrix to Eric Clapton and Muddy Waters, Tupac had something meaningful to say. I tried to imagine where he had gotten this exposure, how he had become so familiar with all of the divergent artists, but was unsuccessful. The picture of him listening to much of this stuff in his mom's apartment did not fit, nor could I see it occurring up in New York among his family or friends up there (whom I would later meet). In fact this is still a mystery to me. The best answer I have managed is that he absorbed it all in the few months of his residence at the apartment. There the large collections of the two older roommates (Richard and John's brother) would have been available to him and played regularly in the apartment.

It wasn't just the variety of music to which Tupac listened that struck me, but the fact that he was genuinely interested in and knowledgeable about that music, and the various artists behind it. Richard played the role of DJ through the discussion, putting on a succession of different records that they would then discuss and critique after hearing only a few bars. I specifically remember Tupac talking about Tracy Chapman. He felt she was a musical genius. After quoting several lyrics from a favorite song of hers, he concluded, "That's a true poet."

Tupac was definitely a sponge of amazing efficacy, particularly with information at all dealing with either of his two loves in life:

rap and acting. As an actor, the ease with which Tupac remembered lines was incredible, and his knowledge of craft impressive. When I asked him one afternoon the type of actor he wished to be, his reply was immediate: "A Shakespearean actor." He said this without emotion, from the windowsill at the fore of the apartment, not breaking his passive yet focused gaze outward.

"A what?!" I replied, taken aback. And he repeated himself. "Why?! They don't make any money." I was thoroughly confused. The Tupac I knew was destined for far greater things than low-budget productions in small playhouses. I envisioned him marching through the entertainment industry to some star-spangled movie or TV career, and untold millions. And I just assumed that his vision for himself was twice as grand as any I could conjure for him. His reply was disappointingly anticlimactic, and downright troubling.

He calmly informed me that Shakespearean actors were the very best in the world. That Shakespeare could not be faked. And that great skill and training were required of those so ambitious as to attempt the material. At that moment I envisioned a painting of him dressed in Renaissance attire, with ruffled collar, tights, and all. I told him of the idea, and that I would call the painting "Shakurspeare." He jokingly stiffened into a formal pose, throwing his nose in the air and following it with his gaze, clutching the rap pad that had been in his hand. I told him to hold the pose and grabbed my own notepad from the coffee table. I did a quick pen sketch to show off my skills. It was the first drawing I did of him. We laughed about it afterward.

This quiet maturity of his, so fundamental a part of his lore, showed itself often, gaining him advocates in interesting places. When as a new student he selected Don McLean's "Vincent" for his acting assignment at age fifteen, the head of the theater department, Donald Hicken (whom Tupac would later credit as the sole person at the school to be genuinely interested and concerned), found it a surprising choice and asked the young student why he had selected the piece. Tupac replied that he related to van Gogh because people did not understand him.

Despite my extensive study of van Gogh in my visual art classes, the mention of his name always evoked in me the same thought: a vision of the sandy blond, middle-aged artist taking a sharp knife to his ear, and the resultant blood flowing down his pale, freckled neck. I had never really thought much more about him. But when I later learned of Tupac's curious assignment from Donald Hicken, I became curious about what it was he saw in this particular piece, this artistic rendering of the historical and personal significance of van Gogh. Reading the piece, I saw the answer. The refrain alone painted a picture that I could feel a young, fifteen-year-old Tupac connecting with strongly.

Tupac saw himself as Vincent, with something to say so incredibly true, in a world so incredibly off course, that no one was prepared to hear it.

Up to this point, the whole time Tupac and I were hanging together, I was hanging at his crib. I had long since met and gotten to know his family, but he had never met any of mine. So I decided to take him around my neighborhood to meet my grandmother. She had already heard so much about him since I would always have to explain where I was spending all of my time whenever I returned home from my frequent stints away. And she had been wanting to meet him.

On a Saturday afternoon we got ready to leave Tupac's apartment to head for the bus stop. On the way out, Tupac made the customary stop at Richard's room. After a couple of seconds I heard the familiar sound, *Schick schick!* like a high-pitched maraca shaken twice. Then it sounded again. And then a single drawn out sound, *Ssshhick!* I started to smile. Not only was he in Richard's change again, but after all this time, he was still trying to be quiet about it.

Richard had a huge glass jug of coins in his room that Tupac often tapped for miscellaneous funds. And the jug was actually a reserve of Richard's reserve change. There had been a tall and broad series of stacks of quarters on Richard's dresser that was the impoverished roommate's initial target. But he had depleted these, and moved onto the more troublesome jug in which were nickels, dimes, and pennies mixed in with the coveted quarters. The quarters were all concentrated at the bottom, so he had to shake up the jug to get to them. A lot of times I would wake up to the sound, either from a nap or in the morning. You could hear it from down the hall. I would say to myself, "He must be going to the bank." He would often hit the bank before stepping out to buy cigarettes or some other small item. I just assumed Richard would eventually approach him about it but he never did. I guess he saw that Tupac didn't have shit. And it wasn't hurting him anyway. That's how Richard was. I could definitely see him writing it off as a karmic investment. He was cool like that.

I remember the first time I saw Tupac utilize this resource. It was under a similar circumstance where we were about to take the bus somewhere. We were heading out the door when I realized we didn't have any bus fare. "Aright," Tupac said dryly, the blank look instantly cloaking his face. He then walked into Richard's room, letting the door close behind him enough so that I couldn't see in clearly. When I heard a jingling sound through the door, I was like, "Damn, he's going in Richard's change." With the same lack of expression on his face he walked out of the room, eyes focused straight ahead, and we headed out the door.

Since then, it had become a regular exercise to me. I had even exploited the resource a couple of times myself; not while Tupac was around. But whenever he left the apartment, the jug was fair game. Change was not the only assistance Tupac silently procured from Richard. Just as he did with John, Tupac looked at Richard's clothes almost as his own. Sometimes before we went out somewhere, Tupac would walk into Richard's room with only his underwear and come out fully dressed, except for shoes, with bus fare jingling in his pocket.

After the routine pit stop, we walked out the apartment. Instead of waiting for the bus, we decided to walk to the subway station up North Avenue. "Yo Darrin, check this out," Tupac said on the way, pointing to his head and smiling. "See my hairline, it's crazy right?" He pulled his hair back from his forehead, more clearly exposing the zigzag along the line where his hair met his forehead. We laughed. Like all brothers back then, Tupac was big on his haircuts. When he got one, it changed him. He would act different after a haircut, acting out more, more sociable. He felt he was truly attractive with a fresh haircut, with everything neatly trimmed, the lines that he always got all over the sides of his head freshly carved, and all of the borders of his hair, from the forehead around to the neck, cleanly shaped up. One time I was hanging out with him and Mouse and they both got haircuts. They just thought they were the shit afterward. They kept looking at their reflections in windows and in any mirrors that we passed. They kept smiling, and jokingly commenting on how good they looked. It got to be pretty annoying.

When we reached Penn North station, we caught the train to the Rogers Avenue station, only two blocks down the street from my grandmother's house. As we approached her house, I saw my cousins sitting on the front steps. "Awww shit," I thought to myself, a little nervous. I knew they would respect my friend. But still, Tupac was wearing his regular uniform of jeans and jean jacket (not a jean suit, but a pair of jeans and a jean jacket made of slightly different cloth, color, and design) written all over with marker. And my cousins were sitting on the bottom steps near the sidewalk, where they could see everything, with more than ample time to formulate jokes and erupt into giggles. I was already the outcast of the neighborhood, with no fly gear and no desire to be on the corner cracking jokes like everybody else. And now I was walking around with someone in wrinkled up, browned-from-use, written-all-over clothes, with a bunch of lines cut in his head that were badly distorted due to his need for a shape-up.

But my cousins remained true to me and we passed without incident. They all spoke politely, and I didn't push my luck by stopping to converse and make introductions. When we got inside I found out my grandmother wasn't home. "Damn." Instead of walking right back out, I told Tupac, "Let's chill for a minute." For as long as we could, we watched TV in the living room. But it was boring as hell so we left after about ten minutes and headed for my mother's house a couple of miles away.

When we stepped up on my mother's porch, I could see her through the screen door, sitting in the living room watching TV. We knocked and walked in. "What brings you around here?" was her cold greeting to us. She just kept watching TV. I was trying to reciprocate to Tupac some of the love he and his mother had shown me, and all my mother could manage was a confrontational utterance, barely acknowledging our presence. "I want you to hear something," I told her. I told her who Tupac was and that I wanted her to hear him rap. She just kept watching TV. After a few moments of silence, "Go ahead," she said. Tupac did "Babies Having Babies" for her. She never looked away from the TV. When he was done, I asked her, "So, what do you think?" She didn't even look up. "It was aright," she said coldly. I could tell beforehand that she wasn't in the mood to turn away from what she was watching and hear someone rap. But this was a friend of mine that I had brought all the way over there, and I thought she could have at least pretended.

"Aright!" I called out. "You ain't *hear* that?!" We just stood there. I felt so embarrassed. Tupac asked me quietly, "You ready to go, man?" It obviously hurt him pretty badly. We left and went back over to my grandmother's, where I was able to offer him the respect and love that he deserved as my good friend. Having since returned home, my grandmother was eager to meet this much talked about friend of mine.

One day a friend of ours from the school, a theater student named Randy Dixon, came over to Tupac's apartment to hang out with us. They were working out on Richard's exercise bar that he kept mounted in the hallway. Richard used the contraption for hanging upside down from special ankle straps. But they were doing chin-ups and walking around the apartment with their shirts off and their chests pumped up like they had the bodies of two Mr. Universes or something, the two theater students putting on a show. Randy was a slender, dark-skinned guy like Tupac, so I guess they felt a bond in that respect. And because of their slender frames, whatever muscle mass they had showed through clearly. So although I was more muscular than both of them, and stronger, they felt theirs was a look I should envy. "Just trying to work out a little, you know," Tupac said to me when I laughed at them for trying to act like they were hot shit. They even went so far as to oil up their bodies with baby oil and pose in front of a mirror, trying to outdo each other. "You should do it too . . . You know . . . get a little cut, like . . . me and Randy," he had the nerve to say to me.

"Fuck y'all," was my only reply.

Seeing himself all oiled up and fully flexed, Tupac was newly inspired to show off his shining black body. He came up with an idea. "Yo, you know what we gonna do?" he said out of nowhere. "We gonna have a toga party." We all liked the idea, and began at once to prepare. We started calling everyone from the school that we could get hold of. We grabbed a bunch of white sheets from both Tupac's and Richard's rooms. I figured, why settle for the same old white sheets, so we got some black paint that was laying around the crib and took everything into Tupac's room to create the phattest togas anyone had ever seen. We took the free-flowing, abstract approach, and just started slinging paint on the sheets. By the time we were finished there was paint everywhere, on everything. The can of paint had tipped over more than once in the midst of the commotion. To let the sheets dry, we hung them on the fire escape outside Tupac's bedroom window.

When it was time, we put on our togas and waited for everyone to arrive. But we must have done a poor job of communicating the theme of the night because no one came in a toga. As more and more people arrived, it became more and more obvious that we were the only ones sitting around in sheets while everyone else was in regular clothes. Tupac caught on early, and quietly snuck off to

Richard's room, returning a couple minutes later in regular clothes. Soon afterward, Randy went into Tupac's room and changed back into his regular clothes. I was pissed by this desertion because I only had the same old raggedy and dirty shorts and T-shirt that I had worn over there the day before. I couldn't wear anything of Tupac's because his clothes were always in a dirty, cigarette smoke–smelling heap on his bedroom floor. He was very sloppy. Once I had put on a shirt of his that seemed to be in decent condition when we were going out somewhere. As soon as we got outside, the smell of cigarettes began to hover about me. And before long, it was overwhelming. I ended up feeling and smelling like a dirty ashtray the whole night. So when I retreated to his room, I begrudgingly changed back into my raggedy clothes. I had no choice. I was looking like a damn fool out there in that sheet.

The party didn't turn out at all as we had planned or hoped. We had had visions of hordes of scantily clothed girls, whirling about at a dizzying freak fest. And at the center of it all would be the three of us, getting our fill. But it didn't turn out that way. The party was a subdued get-together of fifteen to twenty people. We drank a lot, decimating Richard's liquor stores which he had hidden deep in the back of the cabinets under the kitchen sink in order to guard against such infringement, smoked, and had a generally good time. The next morning there were little splotches of black paint all over the apartment. The paint must have been oil-based because it had never fully dried.

One of the few times in our couple years together at the school that I bested my very self-assured, at times arrogant, friend was with a sister named Kelly who was one of the prettiest girls in the school.

Kelly was a dancer in Tupac's year in whom he had been interested since his first year there. She tended to hang with the gay guys in the dance department, and was dating one of them, a dancer named Eskiah. This bothered Tupac. He felt that someone whose preference was not even girls should be no match for him. He always tried to hang out with their crew by the dance studio, talking and joking around with them; all to get close to Kelly, but she paid him no mind. This irked him to no end because he thought that if he tried hard enough, he could get any girl in the school. Even among the more stuck-up, more high-society sisters, he was quietly successful with a few. And Kelly was not that type of girl, though she was more than pretty enough to be if she chose. She was cool, paying no attention to the darker/lighter skin, or privileged/ underprivileged thing. Yet Tupac could make no headway.

For the previously mentioned Spring Fever skit that Gerard and I wrote, entitled, "I Wanna Be Your Man," in which I enlisted Tupac to play the part of the popular jock, I had gotten Kelly to play the jock's girlfriend who I eventually won from him. Our connection (Kelly's and mine) through this mini-production provided the perfect opportunity for us to get to know one another. And I used it liberally, arranging frequent mini-rehearsal sessions with her after school in which we discussed the skit, her lines, and whatever else came up. I called just one rehearsal for the entire crew of the production. But for her and me, I arranged several. It worked beautifully.

During our second or third after-school rendezvous, she asked me about a drawing that I had done for a very good friend of mine named Isha earlier that year. The drawing was bad! It was large and imposing, and brought forth all of the attributes of this beautiful girl like only someone who was truly in love with her could manage. And man, was I in love with Isha, so much so that the thought of telling her as much, and actually trying my hand at it, made me freeze in my tracks. I guess somewhere inside I felt that I didn't deserve someone so perfect. Anyway, Isha had absolutely loved the piece, and proudly showed it around the school. All the girls jocked it. And remembering this, Kelly asked me if I could do one for her. She said she wanted to hang it in her mother's hair salon. At this my adrenaline began to run and I smiled inside. I knew that I likely had her at that point. I would make sure to do a killer job on the drawing, and she would love it.

The finished product was incredible. And her reaction was even more positive, and more gracious than I expected. I told her that I was able to do so good a job because I liked her and had closely studied every feature, every line, every curve of her face. She was so cool; she made it easy for me. "I didn't know you liked me," she said. That was all it took. Just like that, we were an item, spending a lot of time together outside of school, no longer needing the guise of rehearsals.

Besides Eskiah, Kelly had a boyfriend who used to pick her up from school every day. He went to Woodlawn High School out in the county and was a cousin of one of my classmates. So I knew to keep my involvement with her quiet. But in no time she broke up with him and began to come over to my grandmother's house with me after school to talk and hang out before going home. She would catch the subway with me to my grandmother's; then I would catch the bus with her to the northeast side of the city where she lived. I would then catch the same bus back home. What can I say, puppy love drives the underexperienced boy to great lengths.

It was all pretty innocent for a while. We didn't do a whole lot by free-spirited art school standards, just kissed a lot, and rolled around on the couch. She told me about Tupac's courtship. "I don't think he really liked me," she told me. "I think he just wanted to have sex with me." I saw where he had gone wrong.

Brothers in general started to notice all of the time we were spending together and became jealous. But I continued to keep the extent of our relationship a secret. I felt privileged to be in such a relationship with so beautiful a girl, and I didn't want to dirty it up by putting it on the school gossip circuit where all the school idiots could have their way with it.

When I eventually went to her house and we consummated the relationship down in her basement, it became clear to me that she was probably used to more sexual and less thoughtful relationships. I was a little caught off guard by all of the freaky shit she began to say in the heat of it all. I almost started laughing when she repeated numerous times, "It's going through my throat!" These apparent signs of extensive experience she exhibited led me to think she probably found me refreshing, a somewhat innocent guy who showed her a whole new level of respect and consideration.

I kept all of this to myself for the longest. It wasn't until almost a year later that I told Tupac. We had been over at his girlfriend Mary's house and were on the bus stop, headed to his mother's apartment, when he brought up Kelly's name, and how he still wanted her. "Kelly," I said.

"Yeah, wussup with Kelly . . . you ain't do nothin' right?" he asked.

"I hit it," I replied, frankly.

"What?!"

"I said I hit it!" I repeated with bravado, since he had gone out of his way to question me so bluntly. And I knew what he was really saying: "You couldn't have hit it because I wasn't able to."

"Y'all did something?" he asked again, unable to believe it. I was then glad to rub it in.

"I hit it," I said definitively. He just stood there, dazed.

"What's up with y'all now?"

"We cool," I replied with a smile. Kelly and I had dated for only a month or two. When we stopped seeing each other, I just let the whole thing die quietly.

"Man, I gotta hit it . . . I gotta hit it," he said after a short pause. He asked me how it was, and I told him she was mad tight (as in dope, as in tremendous). I gave him an overview of exactly how tremendous she was. I even told him that all he needed to do was to say that he liked her. "Man, I gotta hit it," he kept saying. I could tell the whole story really fucked with him. Not only had he been unsuccessful, but he saw himself as the leader of our crew. And the fact that I had gotten in where he couldn't dealt too big a blow. But with only a couple weeks left in school, I didn't see much chance for him to do anything about it.

However, this is Tupac we're talking about. Not even three days later, he spotted Kelly and Eskiah outside after school. Wasting no time with grandiose schemes or drawn out campaigns, he simply invited Kelly to the apartment to hang out. "Darrin be up there," he said he told her. "Let's just go up there; let's all hang out up there," he said to both of them since Eskiah was cock-blockin' something terrible, and the only way Kelly would come was if Eskiah came also. So he invited them both. When they got to the apartment he rolled a joint, and they all smoked. He had remembered Kelly mentioning once before that she couldn't hold her weed, so he knew this was the key.

Kelly got extremely high, and was loosening up rapidly. He told me that he then started telling her that he really liked her. He said she was like, "Really?" I could tell he remembered every little detail of what I had told him on the bus stop, and used it all skillfully. But Eskiah continued his foiling ways. So Tupac devised a plan. He pulled Eskiah to the side. "Let me fuck Kelly. And I'll let you fuck me," was his proposal. "Hell, yeah," Eskiah replied enthusiastically. "I'll go for that."

The rest Tupac re-enacted for me at the scene of the crime as follows:

> I'm on the bed like this [kneeling on the bottom end of the bed], fuckin' the shit outta Kelly. And she kept saying, "My throat, my throat!" [At this I began to laugh, and told him that I knew for a fact he was telling the truth. Remembering some of the other things she had said, I was like, did she say this? and, did she say that? He replied yes to each. Man! we laughed.] . . . I'm on top of Kelly, 'bout to bust a nut, and Eskiah touched the back of my leg, like, "Okay. When's my turn?" I was like, "Hold up! Hold up! Let me finish first and you get your turn!" smackin' his hand off my leg and shit [still kneeling on the bottom end of the bed, bent forward, smacking at an imaginary hand on his upper thigh]. After I bust my nut, Kelly was just passed out, still high as shit. Eskiah was like, "When's my turn?" So we get to arguing. I told him, "You must be outta your fuckin' mind if you think I'm uh let you do something to me." I told him, "Fuck you. You're crazy." He was all like, *You lied to me,* like a ole bitch and shit, all upset. He got Kelly and stormed out and shit.

Tupac's telling of this story was hilarious. I saw that he would go to practically any length to get what he wanted. Around him, I had grown to not be surprised by virtually anything. He told me that he hooked up with her again, and had her on the bathroom sink.

He tried to act interested in her, but after the second rendezvous, the fact of the matter was, he wasn't. He had conquered, and that was really what it had been about the whole time. Eskiah had returned to school bitter, and went about spreading the false rumor around school that he had fucked Tupac. By the time the year ended, the rumor was all around school. But I knew the truth, and Kelly confirmed what Tupac told me.

Busboys vs. Dishwashers

Tupac's day-to-day pursuit of his most brilliant dreams permeated every facet of his life; he was always working. Regularly, he would slip into some character or other, whether from a show or movie we were watching on television, or simply from among his frequently tapped list of regulars. Without warning he would assume the persona of one of these characters, spinning off entire narratives out of thin air. He would do this all the time, as if he were addicted and couldn't stop. It was natural to him. One of his favorite personas was Tony Montana, Al Pacino's over the top gangster character from *Scarface*. I cannot count the number of hours spent with this harsh, aggressive character and his menacing Cuban accent, the impassioned portrayal of whom produced showers of spittle to be dodged by whatever audience lay in its path. Tupac smashed all barriers in his mind and tapped the deepest reaches of his soul to re-form himself and build anew these characters with meticulous attention to detail. When one's back was turned, one could genuinely be fooled. Another favorite persona was an old drunk whom he would portray with equal dedication and enthusiasm. The life span of these characters, once assumed, could be quite long, often torturously so. It was definitely a hilarious scene to witness, when not painfully annoying.

At the fine dining restaurant where we worked down by the Inner Harbor, Tupac would masterfully imitate an Arab waiter named Saeed. Saeed had a habit of telling "Black" jokes, so we especially enjoyed cracking on him. "Go bus your cousins," he would say to us in his warped English, smiling and pointing to a table of Black customers; he quickly became our favorite work time comic relief. His wonderfully foreign mannerisms, his incorrect English and awkwardly elitist air made him a walking bin of material. And Tupac exploited all of these with surgical precision and thoroughness, imitating him to a T. Tupac was so funny in his portrayal that Saeed could make no meaningful counterattack. He was forced to simply swallow his childish frustration with only looks of disgust to offer in return. This only amused us further. But we worked hard for him when it counted, and he always tipped us accordingly, so there was no serious bad blood between us.

As busboys we made most of our money in tips, collecting twenty to thirty dollars a night, busting our asses in that restaurant. And as busboys we were looked down upon by some of the waiters and waitresses, who resented having to pay us fifteen percent of their tips, while still they demanded of us every bit of energy and effort, expecting us to run around for them like trapped mice in some cruel experiment. In the busy hours it was no fun at all.

No favorites were we of the dishwashers either, who resented the way we would, on occasion, bring back dishes late on busy nights. A lot of times it wasn't our fault as tables would clear faster than we could bus them, but still we were the scorned bearers of the bad news. And then on other busy nights it would be our fault since we would loaf and joke around while the last few tables were finishing. We would be so happy to get a breather after scrambling all night to keep a steady stream of clean tables available, that when the last table was seated and no new ones were needed, it was playtime. Some of the dishwashers, aware of our habits, would repeatedly ask us whenever they glimpsed us going by the kitchen, "Are there any more dishes out there?" knowing full well there were because they hadn't seen us bring back any trays in a while. Sometimes the tension got pretty thick. On one exceptionally busy evening, Tupac, Mouse (whom we had recently gotten a job with us at the restaurant), and I had been bringing back loads of dishes all evening long, yet at the end of the night there were still many tables to be cleared. The dishwashers were not going home any time soon and they knew it. Consequently they began to grow angry. I decided to be Mr. Nice Guy and help them knock out some of the dishes in order to speed things up. Their situation looked bad. Tupac and Mouse, on the other hand, were dragging their feet and joking around out on the floor, waiting for the last table to leave instead of dutifully bringing back everything they could so that the dishwashers would not be inundated at the last minute. I started to understand where the dishwashers were coming from. Their already sour mood took a sharp turn for the worse when the last table finally left and what they had anticipated began in force as Mouse and Tupac let loose the deluge without mercy. All of a sudden they were appearing in the kitchen at dizzying intervals of what seemed to be every few seconds, lugging in a new tray each time laden with haphazardly placed dishes piled high on top of each other. Increasingly bitter about their dramatically worsening situation the dishwashers began to plot against Tupac.

Again, it was Tupac who was singled out, despite the fact that Mouse was equally guilty. Mouse may have been relatively new on the job, but he knew what he was doing. Still, it was Tupac they focused on. I heard the plotters say they were going to "fuck him up" if he brought back another dish. They didn't know that Tupac and I were as close as we were. I immediately turned around to both of them, incensed: "Y'all not gonna do *shit* to Tupac!"

They looked first to each other, shocked and confused by my outburst, and then to me as if I was truly crazy. They asked me what I had to do with it. I replied indignantly: "I have everything to do with it . . . Tupac is my motherfuckin' boy! And like I said, y'all ain't gonna do shit to'm!" I was very loud, and pissed off because here I was trying to help these bastards and they had the nerve to be plotting against my boy right in front of me. In no time I was in the middle of an uproar in the kitchen with both dishwashers in my face talking about how they would whip my ass and how it wasn't my beef anyway. The head cook, Ed, who was the uncle of the two dishwashers, was yelling at us from the cooking line, saying that he wasn't going to stand for any trouble. He told us that if we were going to fight we better go outside, and that if we went outside we better never come back.

My blood raced from head to toe, my heart pumped wildly, and my head throbbed with the colliding thoughts of losing my job, getting my ass kicked by two guys, and any and all possible means of avoiding either or both of these undesirable outcomes. All the while Tupac and Mouse were out in the dining room dawdling around. As I ran through in my mind possible ways to take the two guys out quickly, before they would know what hit them, Tupac finally returned to the kitchen and asked me what was up. I told him they were planning to kick his ass, inching aggressively toward the guys now that I had back. The switch had been thrown inside me, and reason was lost. Tupac held me back and started trying to calm me down, which only increased my anger since he didn't immediately jump to my side and join in. I was the type of quiet guy who is an explosion waiting to happen. And when provoked, I exploded readily, generally to the considerable detriment of whoever was on the receiving end, since my little bit of size and heavy hands proved to be formidable tools on the rare occasions that I found myself using them.

But Tupac had never seen me this way before. Our previous pledges to always have each other's back were probably taken a bit lightly by him. He may have questioned exactly how much help I would actually be if it ever really came down to it. But from this night forward, he knew without question that when I said I had his back, I had his back. We avoided any blows that night, but the tension remained.

A couple weeks later Tupac's cousin Scott came to Baltimore. Looking for a new lease on life well away from the darker side of living in New York City, he was considering staying indefinitely. Taking care of the first order of business, Tupac got him a job as a busboy at the restaurant. Scott was a big, cocky guy (as in muscular), a few years older than us. Once the dishwashers got a load of him they wanted nothing to do with us. All friction was immediately null and void.

Tupac looked up to this older cousin of his to whom he credited his passion for acting. It was Scott who facilitated Tupac's getting the role in the production of *A Raisin in the Sun* up in New York

when they were much younger, the same experience that made Tupac realize with absolute certainty his career path. And Scott's
tenure at the School for the Performing Arts in New York was the
inspiration behind Tupac's choice of the Baltimore equivalent.

Scott was a funny guy who put his dramatic talent to work often,
manifesting out of thin air an unending array of what I thought of
as microcharacters. I guess this is where Tupac got his habit from,
of spontaneously taking on characters. Scott was always contorting
and reforming his face in some new way, along with his speech pat-
terns, personality traits, walk, posture, all to convincingly portray
the presence of some character, chosen at random. Each of these
bursts in character was played out through a unique scenario that
was somehow appropriate for that character. Scott made it his mission to make everyone around him laugh.

Tupac obviously enjoyed having this link to his past there with
him in his present. The two of them had a good time, more often
than not just hanging close to home, smoking herb and drinking,
and tripping on whatever or whoever. But on the job only a few
weeks, Scott was caught stealing red-handed by the owner of the
restaurant and was immediately fired. It all happened after work
one night. John and I were outside waiting, unaware, until they
came out. Tupac didn't want to say anything, and tried not to; he
was embarrassed. But he was pissed! Obviously so, and could not
hide it. Scott walked out the front door with his head down, and
Tupac, behind him, fuming. As we started away from the restaurant, it all came out like thunder: "What the *HELL* were you thinking?!" Tupac boomed at Scott. The older, unusually large cousin
collapsed within himself even further, remaining quiet, unable to
look anyone in the eye. I asked what was going on and Tupac filled
us in with a highly sensationalized, humorously (to John and my-

self) ad-libbed interpretation of the events. He was as angry as I had ever seen him. Apparently the owner himself had caught Scott with his hand in the upstairs cash register.

Unwisely, Scott tried to offer explanation. His first lame attempt was that his hand had fallen into the register. This he quickly followed with an equally ridiculous idea, that he was actually putting money *in* the register. Both of these were only kerosene to Tupac's fire. Tupac was without question the older cousin that night. He displayed no deference toward the obviously guilty older relative, taming none of his biting comments.

The whole way home Scott attempted to explain himself. "Man, fuck them," he tried to say, pulling the "us against them," family card.

"*Fuck* them?! . . . You idiot! I gotta work there!" Tupac replied.

The verbal bludgeoning persisted through the entire walk home, sparking anew every time Scott said even a word. It was unrelenting, and Scott was pitiful. Arguing a point had always been an art form to Tupac. That night he worked a masterpiece.

 **Prom Night**

In 1988 the senior prom was more like a schoolwide party than a prom. It reminded me of the Beaux Arts Ball, except with tuxedos and dresses instead of costumes. Few came with "real" dates. There were almost no unfamiliar faces. And there were as many non-seniors in the crowd as seniors. Tupac was one of them. He came with a group of students who all went stag. One of the girls in his group rented a limousine that would serve as their party chariot throughout the evening. When Gerard and I arrived with our dates they were already there, turning the party out.

My evening wouldn't go so well as theirs. I had gone back and forth with a girl in the dance department whom I was going to take, and then I wasn't, because she was being wishy-washy about our arrangements, and then again, a couple days before, we were on. The mood between us was strained and I was unhappy with my decision the entire time. The truth is, I regretted not asking Isha. I had taken her the previous year, and feared it would be too much to ask her again. She was out there on the dance floor with everyone else, having fun. I was miserable.

Gerard and I arrived with our dates at the Belvedere Hotel on Biddle Street where the affair was being held in a huge ballroom on the first floor. Without walking around we immediately took a seat at one of the tables along the wall where I remained with my date almost the entire night, looking out at everyone else having fun: *Why didn't I just go by myself like everyone else!?* I thought. Although he had no date, Tupac managed to dance the whole night. He even made his way over to Isha at one point, and danced with her for a little while. This really made me lament my situation, and my decision. I wanted out of my evening commitment. My date was exceptionally fine, but she was boring as hell. So after having remained seated far too long, I got up, leaving my date at the table, and went out to the dance floor to join Tupac and other friends. But I was only up a short while before everyone, having had their fill of the event, began to leave en masse.

The next stop was a house party out by Edmonson Village. One of the dancers, Tonya Jeffries, was throwing it and everyone was going: white, Black, it didn't matter that night, despite it being probably the first time the white kids had been anywhere near the area. Now *this* was a good time. Your typical eighties, around the way house party: pitch black furnitureless basement turned sauna, with two huge amplifiers on either side of a DJ table at the front of the room. A minilamp illuminating the mixing equipment on the table provided the only light in the place.

I figured the prom was over. When we arrived at the party, I went off on my own. Any date-related obligations were at that point null and void as far as I was concerned. I saw Isha and pulled her aside. I told her that I was having a miserable time, and that I wished I had asked her instead of the girl I took. She just smiled and asked me why I hadn't. I was floored. I told her that Tupac was having a party at his apartment afterward, and then asked Gerard to *please* take my date home whenever he was ready to leave. Then I jumped on the dance floor and started to get in some of the dancing I had missed at the prom. But before too long many were ready to settle down and get comfortable, away from any chaperone presence. So the vibe shifted to Tupac's apartment, where he was hosting the after-hours set in a more laid back and unsupervised flow. Gerard obliged my request and drove my date home. I hopped in the limo with Tupac and his crew for the ride over to his apartment. Richard was out of town for the week so the apartment was wide open. Finally, I would have some fun.

It was late, around one o'clock in the morning, when we tromped into Tupac's. I already had an assortment of clothes over there, since I almost lived there anyway, so I immediately changed into some shorts and a T-shirt; Tupac did the same. Many others had brought a change of clothes, and followed suit. Slowly, people trickled in from Tonya's, some carrying six-packs of beer and various bottles of different kinds of liquor. And Tupac was generous with Richard's stash, placing a couple open bottles out on the coffee table, and inviting all to the beers in the fridge.

The living room area in the front of the apartment remained the focal point of the party the entire night. Everyone congregated there, making only short trips to the bathroom, and to the kitchen for beers and ice. As more people walked through the door, the pile-up in the living room continued without release to the deeper reaches of the apartment. After a while we were all loosely sprawled over the couch, chairs, and floor, calmed by the effect of the various mind- and mood-altering substances, sitting on top of one another, some talking calmly, others squawking at the top of their lungs as if their intention was to annoy. I still hadn't built up much of a tolerance for alcohol so I got pretty drunk. Feeling a little worn, cramped, and tired of the loud mass of simultaneous voices pushing each other higher, I quietly made a move to Tupac's room in the back. Isha didn't come after all, so I was a little depressed, and very unimpressed with just about everybody there. Numb and at peace I laid down on Tupac's bed, propping myself up against the wall and taking little sips from the concoction I had carried with me.

As I expected, and quietly hoped, a couple heads dangling long hair peeked in the door and then entered. It was Lisa, in whom I was somewhat interested, and Rebecca, in whom I was not at all. They were giggling and pushing through the door with much of the silliness I had purposefully escaped. I dryly responded to their attempts at upbeat humor, and lay there unhappy, not wanting them to leave (at least not Lisa) but definitely wanting them to transform. They were up to something, and before I knew it my drink had spilled and I was wrestling both of them on the floor of the room, trying to keep on my shorts that they were trying to pull off. I was a little surprised when after a minute or so, they were still going strong, showing no sign of letdown. Rebecca grabbed a pair of scissors from Tupac's dresser and started trying to cut my shorts off. Finally, Tupac came into the room and jumped into the fray, proclaiming, "I got your back, Darrin," as if it was his gentlemanly duty to do so. Evening out the odds, he grabbed Rebecca and carried her off. I then subdued the other half of the sex-crazed duo, and commenced to kissing her as we grinned back and forth at each other. After only a few moments, Lisa and I noticed a strange silence across the shadowy room and looked over. We could see the silhouette of Tupac laying on the floor and that of Rebecca's head with her hair dangling forward, bobbing up and down over him. We were shocked, especially since Lisa had just confided in me that she was acting as an emissary for Rebecca, who was interested in me. At this we just laughed to ourselves. Not long afterward Tupac got up quietly and left the room without a word. This scene was probably the craziest thing I had ever witnessed. But judging from the many stories of his in which he would detail to me his various exploits in and about the school, it was certainly not so ground-breaking to Tupac.

In the morning I awoke in Tupac's bed with the two girls on either side of me. I couldn't remember how the night had ended, so I had no idea how I had ended up there. When I stirred, it woke Lisa, and we finished what we started the night before, despite the fact that Rebecca was right beside us. After Rebecca's incredible indiscretion with Tupac, I was not much worried about what she would think or how she might react. When I finally walked out into the living room it was full of people still asleep, laid out all over the place. I was kind of shocked that everyone was still there. When everyone began to get up, I found out that there had developed at some point during the night a plan to go to King's Dominion Amusement Park. Shortly thereafter we all piled into three cars for the three-hour drive down to Virginia to King's Dominion, where we spent all day and had a ball.

Off to
the Bronx

School was over for the year, I had graduated, and Tupac, having successfully completed his second year, would be a senior in the fall. With school out of the way it was all about working down at the restaurant and rhyming, all about Born Busy, or as we would say, "the Born Busy sound." When not at work our time was spent writing and reciting rhymes, practicing our timing and collaborative flow. But as the summer progressed, Tupac became restless; he wanted to return "home." After making loose mention of his desire to visit New York on several occasions, he reached a certain resolve one day a month or so into the summer and asked me if I wanted to join him. I didn't hesitate in responding. I had never been to New York before and found the possibility exciting. Plus, I was going to be attending college there in the fall, so I wanted to start getting familiar with the vibe. That same day we called in to the restaurant and informed them that we would not be coming in, ever. We each had our last checks (still uncashed) and a small wad of tip money, and we were going to New York. Tupac was very anxious to return to his roots, to that other reality from which he had come and from which he drew so much of his energy and charisma. He loved New York and quickly infected me with his enthusiasm. We set our departure date for only three days away.

Without delay we went about preparing. No word from him was necessary; I could sense what it all meant and worked equally hard in our rehearsal sessions in the days following. We spent hours practicing rhymes over and over again, revisiting old ones and hammering out new ones, readying ourselves for the challenges sure to come.

By this time, we were extremely well practiced, and were comfortable reciting our rhymes anywhere, in front of anyone. On the back of the bus one night on the way home to Tupac's apartment we were discussing our rhymes as usual. We didn't care that the bus was full of people. We knew they were all listening. Actually, having an audience kind of pumped us up. We kept talking as if the bus were empty. "Remember how we did the rhyme yesterday? 'We work *hard!* to give you rhymes' . . . You know, really stressing it, together?" we would say, for instance.

"Oh, y'all rap?" someone near us asked.

"Yeah, you know . . ." we responded proudly. Someone else then asked where we were from. Tupac immediately responded, "New York. We going to New York tomorrow, for a couple of days, to do some things," he added, insinuating some greater purpose for our trip beyond just visiting. A couple of folks then asked us to recite something. We were happy to oblige, and kicked a couple of things. Everyone was very impressed. Even up in the front, they were into it, calling back compliments. "Y'all good. Y'all gonna make it some day," the driver called back to us. "Now keep the noise down," he added with a smile. Everybody laughed. What impressed them all so much was our timing, our collaboration, and also our conviction. We were serious. And we didn't make a single error through the whole exhibition, comfortably exploring all of the different nuances of the delivery: the drawn out words, the stressed ones. We had practiced so much that we probably wouldn't have been able to mess up if we tried. Proud and confident, we exited the bus at Park Avenue; everyone had liked our flow, and offered nothing but the most positive vibes and well-wishes. I remember thinking that we should have passed around a hat and made a couple bucks. We were ready for New York.

The morning that we were to leave we boarded the number 28 bus that would take us from Tupac's apartment down to the Grey-hound station, where we would catch a bus to New York. Boarding the number 28, we walked to the back as we always did despite there being only a couple passengers on the bus, and dove into the very last seats. I grabbed the corner seat by the window on the left and Tupac the opposite window seat on the other side. A few stops later two guys a little older than we were boarded the bus and walked to the back. One of the guys was someone I knew from my old neighborhood and we spoke. After speaking to me, this same guy started to look at Tupac up and down as if to size him up; apparently the way in which Tupac and I were seated did not convey our close association. He seemed to be checking out Tupac's jean ensemble, the same colorfully written over outfit he wore so often. The guy asked Tupac if he had an extra cigarette. "Yeah," Tupac replied, tapping one loose from his pack. Figuring the guy was cool since he knew me, Tupac moved more quickly than usual, as a sign of respect. The guy paused for a second; and then for no apparent reason:

"Naw, I don't want this shit!" He plucked the cigarette back in Tupac's face. In one motion Tupac caught and threw the cigarette back at him, needing no instant to gather the situation, almost as if he had expected it, as if it were some sort of well known, sordid routine. The guy called Tupac a "coon" as I shouted out that Tupac was my boy, fully ready to throw down, which I thought was inevitable at that point. But the guy's buddy quickly acted to defuse the explosion in progress, angrily telling his friend that he needed to "cut that dumb shit out." Looking at Tupac, the guy's reply was, "Fuck him."

"Fuck you!" Tupac yelled back, looking the guy directly in his face; but they got off at the next stop. I was shocked and bewildered by the way this intensely bad energy had just come at him out of nowhere, for no apparent reason. I couldn't understand why he was bucked on by a total stranger to whom he was even being nice. Again came the blank look. We didn't even validate the scene with talking, but just went back to looking out the windows. The rest of the bus ride I tried unsuccessfully to make some kind of sense of this most senseless incident.

That someone would disrespect Tupac in such a way, and for no reason at all, was unsettling to me. It was definitely foul, and disturbing, but Tupac knew I had his back. We had discussed such theoretical situations as this before, agreeing on the importance of sticking together and of remaining unmoved in the moment of truth. We both felt strongly about there being no room within a friendship for "punk shit."

We arrived at the bus station and still there was no utterance of the incident. It obviously bothered him but he was very much focused on getting to New York. After so rocky a start, it seemed that everything simply had to go smoothly from then on. Over the course of the three-and-a-half-hour trip up, we talked and wrote rhymes the entire way. We were in full gear: Tupac in his favorite graffiti'd jean outfit, and me in a pair of shorts and polo shirt both of which matched my wiped-clean tennis shoes. We were pumped, one, to be getting out of Baltimore; and two, to be heading to the very birthplace and nerve center of rap. In the back of our minds was a very real expectation to run into some record executive, or to be heard by someone powerful in the industry and get signed on the spot. We were completely ignorant of the true workings of the music business.

As soon as we emerged from the Holland Tunnel on the New York side, Tupac instantaneously transformed into my personal tour guide; he was brimming with excitement. As we pulled into the terminal at Port Authority he was the first to jump up from his seat and the first to exit the bus. You might have thought that he was on some kind of tight schedule or something. We moved through the station at such speed that I could do nothing but keep up. He reveled in this position of power, disregarding my attempts at asserting myself through question, plunging constantly forward. In a dizzying blur we hurried through corridors, down filthy stairwells into foul stagnant air, waited in line to buy tokens, squeezed through turnstiles, and rushed onto some of the dirtiest looking subway trains I could ever have imagined. I loved every second of it. When the last of the two trains we caught to get out to the Bronx rose above ground, he immediately switched back into tour-guide mode. His enthusiasm cannot be overstated. Breathing in the thick summer air of New York, Tupac was transformed, like Popeye after a can of spinach. He was home.

From the train we stepped onto a well-weathered old platform that looked like a throwback from some old Harlem movie like *The Cotton Club*. The platform was elevated and I could see out over the surrounding neighborhoods that appeared to be more a string of sprawling tenement complexes. The buildings were broken down with busted out windows; many appeared to be abandoned. And in between were open plots of dirt, cluttered over with refuse and suffering patches of badly beaten grass trying desperately to hang on. Taking in this panorama, I tried but saw nothing of the magic and glamour that Frank Sinatra sung so convincingly about in all of those "I Love New York" commercials I was seeing at the time.

The sun beat down relentlessly on everything, heating up the air so that it stuck to our skin. We walked down a rickety-looking stairwell to the street, and around the corner to an apartment building situated next to one of the ragged dirt lots. Tupac hopped up the cement steps of the stoop and I followed. Inside we continued up several flights of stairs in a thin hallway, poorly lit by a small window between each floor level. At the third and last level he walked forward from the stairwell without pausing, straight to the door in the corner to our left, and knocked. As soon as the apartment door opened the warm welcome began. After stepping across the threshold he quickly suggested in my ear, "Don't this remind you of *Good Times?*" To this I wanted to bust out laughing, because in addition to there being too many people squeezed into the small apartment, the children (his cousins) consisted of two boys and a girl, just as in the show. Dutifully, he introduced me to everyone in the apartment and we went straight outside into the neighborhood. He didn't want to waste a second. It seemed like he planned to make up in a couple days what he had missed in the year or more since his last visit. And he was eager to see if everything was still the way he re-membered it.

As we walked through the street, people called out to him in their deep New York accents, and he replied in kind, his voice sounding very different from the one he had been using up until that point, increasingly so with each new person we passed. Every-one was genuinely happy to see him. At a playground around the corner we ran some ball for a little while. The fire hydrant on the corner was open and kids splashed about in the water. We spent the whole day out there, talking to all of his friends and hanging out. Everyone was very pleasant and accommodating to me as the new guy from out of town, and made sure that I was included in every way. But I was preoccupied, in a daze, soaking in the uncom-fortably foreign surroundings. I consciously refrained from saying much of anything at all. With all of the vernacular and foreign twists on pronunciation swirling around me, it was obvious that, al-though I understood perfectly what was being said, I did not know the language. From the few words that did escape, I was asked more than once if I was "from the country." Tupac, on the other hand, was home. In New York he actually fit in, as opposed to Baltimore where he seemed to stick out like a sore thumb.

Into the evening the gathering of friends slowly transformed into a cipher, and the rhyming began. Tupac and I hit a couple of songs, and before long two female MCs challenged us to a little battle . . . It was on. After they recited their rhyme, we answered with "You're a Hot Bitch," which I originally wrote for Jada and Linda. As usual we rocked it, this time taking special care to accentuate the humor-ous nature of the rhyme, as humor always seemed to be the most effective tactic to employ when battling girls. Our challengers themselves couldn't help but laugh at the funny lyrics: "You're a hot bitch! / Are you uh sista or tryin'? / You're a hot bitch! / So hot your draws fryin' / You're a hot bitch / All up in someone's face / And the space between your legs is like a fireplace / You're a hot bitch!" The girls didn't even try to come back. After we hit a couple more rhymes, everyone, including our defeated combatants, began to chant our choruses with us, and ask us to revisit lyrics each time we finished a song. Tupac had made a successful return home, and I had played an important role; but this was just the beginning.

The street began to darken and the group slowly dispersed. As we walked from the playground down to Fordham Road, a couple of Hispanic guys called out to Tupac from across the street and headed toward us. I loved the fact that such a diverse array of people from so many different cultural backgrounds shared the same community. This was very different from what I had known all my life in Baltimore, where you didn't find much more than the basic Black and white back in that day, even across communities.

The two boys were all smiles as they crossed the street, not waiting to reach us before firing off multiple questions in rapid succession: "Yo where you been? Wussup man? When you get back?" Embracing him affectionately, they continued the barrage, not allowing him time to answer. They then looked to me with equal warmth, prompting Tupac to introduce me. I shook hands with both of them, and it was all love from then on.

"Whatchall' doin'? Let's hang out," they suggested, and we agreed without hesitation, walking off with them down the street. A block down Fordham Road we came to a strange-looking mini-supermarket in the middle of an otherwise normal-looking city block. The market was open-faced to the sidewalk with a wide assortment of fresh produce laid out from end to end; I had never seen such a thing. They walked into the establishment between the boxes of oranges on one side and apples on the other without discussion, as if it had been the destination from the beginning. I just followed, taking in the strange arrangement of the store that seemed very much out of place in the middle of the block. They picked up a cigar and a couple forty-ounce bottles of Colt 45 and walked up to the register, paid for the items, and walked right back out, not missing a beat. I had no idea what was going on but this fact neither shocked nor surprised me; I knew enough to expect not to understand a great deal of what I would see over the next few days. I just followed behind, happy to be a party to it all, whatever it was.

We walked around the corner from the store and over to a large white apartment building on a side street off the main strip. The three of them continued to talk and laugh, catching up on old times. Periodically the two new guys shifted the focus to me, shooting off a succession of questions. And with every joke and funny account, without fail, they both looked to me upon delivery of the punch line, engaging me personally in the humor. I could feel their sincerity, and it made me very comfortable. Tupac couldn't have seemed any happier.

After we posted up alongside the building one of the guys pulled out the cigar and carefully ripped it open, creating a perfect tear down the length of it, and poured out the contents. I was completely confused at this point, and looked as much. Looking up to me and noticing the perplexity in my expression, he smiled, but said nothing, and returned to the task at hand. He placed the cigar shell in his shirt pocket and produced from his shorts a little baggy of what I gathered to be herb, and emptied it into the cupped palm of his hand. I continued to watch, intrigued. When he was done, which required only a few moments, the herb had been mashed up, deseeded, and finely rolled into a new cigar; this, I had never seen or even heard of before. It would be a couple more years before I would become familiar with the term "blunt," and realize that that's what those cats were doing back then. Finally he rolled with equal speed a huge spliff to follow the main course.

Ceremonially they handed me the blunt, reciting inflated and exaggerated words and gestures of welcome, stating very officially that it was only right that I have the honorary first toke. The roller of the fine piece of craftsmanship held a lighter to the edge of the blunt now dangling between my lips as if I were the honored guest at some fine restaurant. They looked on approvingly as I got it started with quick puffs like I had seen done with cigars in the movies. Before I knew it we were each taking deep drags from the refashioned cigar, gulps from the forty-ounce bottles, and time slowed, and then blurred. I don't even remember the spliff being started though I'm sure I took hits. All I remember is them laughing with me about the difficulty I was having and Tupac becoming quite upset, transitioning into the role of guardian. I can recall little else from the rest of our time out there that night. When Tupac finally got me back to the apartment I was in such a way that I had to crawl up the stairs. It was late. He spread some blankets on the floor where we would be sleeping and laid me down. After asking if I was okay, to which I grunted I was, he went back outside, returning repeatedly through the night to check on me, only to go right back out. There was this cute girl on the block that he had been after since our arrival. I knew that she was behind his restless darting in and out all night; but I gave it little thought. I was just happy to be comfortably unconscious; all curiosity was put on hold until the morning.

When I awoke to the bright light of a new day, bodies had appeared out of nowhere. It was as if the floors and walls had birthed these people overnight, and more continued to enter the small apartment as the morning progressed. As soon as I opened my eyes I felt the need to get up and get out of the way; I was in the middle of someone's living room, for goodness sake.

There were numerous uncles, aunts, and cousins that hadn't before been seen. I met everyone, Tupac's cousin Kenny in particular. Apparently we would be hanging out with him that day. He was a little older than us and had assumed responsibility for my receiving the "real" New York experience. But for the time being it was all about breakfast. Intensely concerned with my welfare and enjoyment, as everyone had been since I first set foot in the neighborhood, Kenny searched about the kitchen area with Tupac for something to prepare so that I could start things off properly. They whipped up some eggs and toast and we inhaled it all in short order, Kenny telling me the whole time about all the dope things we would be doing, how I would *see New York that day*!

After hanging around the apartment into the early afternoon, listening to music and joking with the various family members, we headed out into the hot sun toward the subway station. Walking past the basketball courts, Kenny split off and headed over to a guy standing against the fence enclosing the courts while Tupac and I waited. They casually made a short-lived transaction before he rejoined us. We continued on to the station. Though quite naïve relative to my present company, I had an idea of what had just occurred; but I couldn't fully assess it. Tupac's complete lack of interest in the whole affair made me pretty certain it wasn't an herb purchase. Nothing was said, or even acknowledged. When we arrived at the station the train was approaching so we darted up the steps and over the turnstiles in a fluid motion so natural that my shock had no time to escalate into fear or question. I just laughed, once safely aboard the train, along with the two of them who looked smilingly to me, enjoying very much what they saw. Not once that day did we pay the fare. Although we would employ smoother tactics from then on, simply pulling back the turnstiles just far enough and walking through as regular as the summer day was bright!

Although we were headed for the Village, we got off well before it so that I could "see New York." Through countless winding little streets and grand avenues we walked, always looking, through various stores, a used record shop, a fenced-in basketball court adjacent to a bustling Manhattan intersection, many different restaurants. After what must have been well over an hour we stopped for a bite to eat at an Italian spot in the Village, and then continued past NYU to Washington Square Park where we were to meet up with two foreign girls that Kenny had met from somewhere. My first impression of the park was one of a shady place, and this did not change as we walked deeper into it. There were all sorts of different drug paraphernalia lying about, used up and broken on the ground. I noticed hypodermic needles, glass pipes, little plastic vials, even a couple of spent condoms. And there were plenty beaten up and not so beaten up individuals spanning what seemed to be several levels of socioeconomic strata, bumbling about with eyes open but obviously unconscious, like the living dead. Kenny knew several of these people, and seemed to know his way around the park quite well.

He quickly spotted the girls and led us over to them. They were relatively attractive: English girls, both of good height and both about Kenny's age, probably a little older. One was a redhead with freckles. She was the healthier of the two, with full breasts and a nice backside. The other was a brunette with short hair and a nose ring; she was a little on the skinny side. Both girls were wearing jeans and a tank top, with sandals. They seemed very pleased to see Kenny; he must have made quite an impression on them. I got the impression that the park had played an important role.

Both of the girls were openly friendly, harboring no pretense or reservation. When it became clear that Kenny was somehow committed to the skinny one, Tupac was visibly pleased, and began to favor her friend. Much more a reserved personality than my two comrades, I hung back, giving them space to do their thing, although the girls had more than enough personality and energy to keep us all well engaged. They never let me drift very far.

Through the rest of the day we continued our frolicking around the Village and surrounding areas, slowly making our way northward. As the sun was beginning to set, we went to Central Park, strolling along its pathways lethargically, a little tired from all of the walking. At one point we stopped for a spell and watched an endless stream of rats jumping off a little bridge passing over the walkway and into a group of bushes at its side.

By the time we got back to the apartment it had been dark for some time. Tupac had been working doggedly on the redhead and had pretty well secured her. We all sat around the kitchen table and talked into the late hours of the night, joking with everyone that came through.

When we laid down to sleep, Kenny, the brunette, and I settled down on the floor in the living room; Tupac and the redhead went into one of the rooms where there were already several people sleeping. I was never quite sure exactly how many people were in the apartment at a given time; it was very strange. After a while Tupac emerged from the room and went back outside. I guess he wasn't finished hanging out; or he was still after that other girl. I

felt Kenny nudge me, and looked up to see him smiling at me, nod-
ding his head toward the room. I knew what he was suggesting, and
just shook my head in refusal. But I couldn't help but smile at the
thought. I hadn't needed even a second to discern the meaning in
his voiceless proposal, probably because I was already thinking the
same thing. Kenny persisted with his mischief, assuring me that the
move would present no shock to the very friendly girl. "Yo, word is
bond. Trust me," he whispered to me, trying to sound as serious as
he could under the circumstances. I was nervous as hell, and wished
I could back out, but there was no way I was going to come off like
a punk in front of this new friend of mine. So with no plan at all, I
got up and walked into the room. Tiptoeing through the others in
the room, I spotted the red locks and laid down next to her, behind
her. I didn't really have to do anything else. She just pushed back
against me, and opened up to me. It was crazy, because there were
others in the room, but I figured if Tupac hadn't cared . . . When I
finished, I just got up and went back out to where I had been laying
down. Kenny gave me a quick thumbs up and went back to sleep. I
slept like a baby.

The next morning Kenny took advantage of the first possible opportunity when we were alone to bring up what had happened. Tupac kind of caught feelings about the whole thing, and got a little
upset. We just laughed him off. It was a little weak of him to get upset over this girl like she was his girlfriend or something. Taking the
blame off me, Kenny told him that he put me up to it because he
knew the girl would be down.

That morning I was further shocked by the strange dynamic of
the curious apartment. When I stood outside the bathroom, waiting to enter, an older man whom I hadn't seen before came out,
spoke politely, and disappeared through a door next to the bath-

room that I had written off as a closet. I found out this was Tupac's uncle, the owner (or primary renter) of the apartment. And he and his wife had, for all intents and purposes, back there in the master bedroom, an apartment unto themselves from which everyone else was strictly forbidden. I guess that was their rightful due, having provided refuge for so many.

Still early in the morning, I walked out of the apartment and down to the pay phone on the corner, where I called my aunt and uncle (actually my great uncle, my grandmother's brother) who lived not far from where we were . . . or so I thought. My aunt owned a couple of beauty shops in the area, so I would first walk over to see her at her shop, and then make my way back up to see my uncle. Already slated to return to New York in the fall for school at the School of Visual Art, I thought it a good idea to familiarize myself with my only family in the area, especially since I would probably need a place to stay. Tupac's uncle's place was at 180th Street and my aunt's beauty shops at 163rd. Seventeen blocks, I figured: no big deal. I told Tupac and Kenny that I was going to see my family and that I was fine. "Naw, I'm straight," I replied confidently, seeing no need to bother them with the simple details. I told them that I would see them either later that night or the next morning, and walked out.

Oh, how sorry I was. Never had I walked so far before in my life. Not only are New York City blocks like no other, but the difference between 180th street and 163rd, I found out, is far from seventeen blocks. I didn't count on all of the unnumbered streets along the way. I just kept walking like I knew where I was going, so as not to look as stupid as I felt; but all the while I became more and more angry with myself the longer the trip dragged on. By the time I made it to my aunt's shop, much of the day was gone and I was worn out. Although I had told my uncle earlier that I would be by to see him, I had no trouble swallowing the morsel of my remaining pride and called him again, admitting to my foolishness in its entirety and asking to be picked up. He was more than happy to do so.

After picking me up from the shop, he took me on a tour of the entire city, as can only be accomplished by automobile. From Yankee Stadium to Wall Street, I saw it all. And he treated me to an unbelievable steak dinner; I hadn't eaten that well in some time. I ended up staying the night with them. As I awoke atop the ample mattress of a luxurious queen-size bed, amid all of the wonderful comforts of home, I realized that I was not at all excited about returning to blankets on a hard floor, Oodles of Noodles, and no phone, as was awaiting me at Tupac's. I was ready to go home. When I returned to Tupac's that afternoon I told him as much. We hung out around the neighborhood that night and returned to Baltimore the following morning. We had crammed a lot into a very few days.

The Show: Our Dream of a Break

We had been hearing of the big Salt-N-Pepa tour, "A Salt with a Deadly Pepa," for some weeks. It was all over the radio. To us Salt-N-Pepa were the tightest female rappers in the business, so we had every intention of going. However, with no money and no connections, the prospect looked increasingly bleak. The evening before the show our situation had not improved. We had no money, no tickets, and no plan. There was no other show that summer we wanted to see more than this one, and the opportunity appeared to be slipping away; but still we were undaunted. Not only did we want to see these iconic figures of the rap world do their thing, but we viewed the show as our big chance to be discovered. Once inside the show, we would get someone to listen to us. And once given an audience, there would be no denying us.

Born Busy had been growing as a group through the summer.

Numerous times the four of us had all gotten together over Gerard's house and spent many hours in his room, working out raps, experimenting with beats, and making recordings. We were ready. So finely tuned were we that we could turn it on instantaneously, at the highest level. All we needed was that audience, a couple minutes of someone's time, and there was no way they would not be blown away. We had no doubt that we would somehow manufacture such an audience. But first we had to get in.

That night Tupac and I hung out over at his mom's apartment. All we thought about was the show, trying to find an answer to our problem. We talked to Mouse and then to Gerard. No one had any ideas. At bedtime Tupac and I laid out blankets on the hardwood floor of the living room and turned out the lights. The half-dim streetlamp, cracked from multiple BB-gun shots, flickered through the front window beyond our heads. We were too anxious to sleep. Tupac suggested that we pray. The words sounded funny out of his mouth, but he was not joking. We folded our hands, closed our eyes, and began to pray. With every ounce of our beings we asked God for a way into the show, and for a meeting with Salt-N-Pepa, making sure to stress exactly how much it would mean.

The next morning, the morning of the show, we received a phone call from Gerard. Unbelievably, his mother had come across four tickets to the show through a friend of hers. Even before he had finished his spiel, we began to bombard him with the full ramifications of the call, that we had even prayed, with the utmost sincerity, for some resolution to our problem. Without hesitating we called up Mouse and gave him the good news.

That day was filled with rehearsing, one song after another: Mouse would come in here; we would transition from this song to this song here; etc. At around nine o'clock in the evening Tupac and I set out for Gerard's house. When we arrived, Gerard and Mouse were seated in the living room waiting. Tupac and I took a seat on the couch. Gerard's father drove us down to the Civic Center (near the Inner Harbor) where the show was being held. Overly excited, we must have looked at our tickets a hundred times on the way down. They had COMPLIMENTARY written very conspicuously on the front; we were special.

When we pulled up to the front of the large event center, hordes of teenagers were swarming all around, most of them hard-looking hip-hop kids from various neighborhoods around the city. Everybody was sporting their new or wiped clean sneakers, with jeans and T-shirt to match. In those days kids were getting shot and killed for their sneakers, and other popular clothing items. But we weren't thinking about any of that. We were on a mission.

After jumping out of the car we walked straight to the front doors, past all of the kids hanging out in front trying to be seen, trying to be hard. Proudly we produced our COMPLIMENTARY tickets and carefully placed the precious stubs in our pockets. Once inside, the building opened up beyond our expectations. It was the first time inside for each of us and we were all humbled. Through the corridor we walked to an entranceway into the inner concert area to which we had been directed. Just as we turned into the entranceway we were rushed by a group of guys, thugged out in urban apparel. They ran up on Tupac and me, smiling and shouting loudly, our names and other greetings. It was a number of the guys from the late-night battle down at Hopkins Plaza, about half of the twenty that had been there that night.

"Yo, y'all should be up *there*!" a couple of them said, pointing up to the huge, brilliantly lit stage in the distance before us. A couple times they repeated this sentiment, serious about what they were saying. Of course Tupac and I enjoyed the flattery tremendously. Mouse and Gerard were completely at a loss. After exchanging our greetings and embraces, and bidding our homeboys good-bye, we filled Mouse and Gerard in on the way to the seats. They remembered our spirited account of the strange evening, and quickly understood.

Our seats were up in the bleachers directly in front of the stage. I liked the view. Looking down on the stage we could see everything. Though their position was said to be superior, it seemed to me that those on the floor couldn't see half of what was plainly within our view. It was my first time at any sort of a concert and I was pleased.

Tony Terry was the first to take the stage, and then Kid 'N Play. The vibe was wild. We stood up the entire time, swaying to the music and participating fully. At first I had to continually look around me, taking notes so as to consciously blend in with all of the obviously experienced concert goers around me; but then I got into it, and it came naturally. Next up was Heavy D. His hits at the time were "Overweight Lover," and "Mr. Big Stuff." I was surprised by the agility with which he moved across the stage, dancing up a storm as if he were some kid half the size. Heavy rocked it but we were waiting for Salt-N-Pepa. When it came time for the headliners, Spinderella, Salt-N-Pepa's DJ, was the first to come out. With a slight gesture to the cheering crowd she climbed up onto the DJ stand at the back of the stage. At this the cheering intensified. Purposefully, she went about getting her equipment in order, and without warning launched a merciless scratch assault that left us all with our jaws hanging open. This was the new Spinderella that had only recently joined the crew. Her unbelievable exhibition seemed to be a little too incredible. I figured at least part of it had to be a recording. It just seemed impossible that she was really doing it all "from scratch," right before our eyes; but maybe this was due more to my lack of familiarity with DJing at such a level. If the exhibition was true and pure, as it very well could have been, I can only apologize because it was simply too hard to believe. All of us kept looking at each other, laughing with disbelief and shaking our heads, one minute absolutely astounded, the next simply refusing to believe. Salt-N-Pepa then burst on stage to their big hit at the time, "Push It." Everyone went crazy. They gave it up that night. My first concert experience was hype; but still we had not achieved the all-important connection.

After the show, back outside the building, we noticed a crowd gravitating toward the hotel down the street; we followed. On our way we saw Kid 'N Play walking in the same direction, behind a barrier set up along the block for the performers. We caught up to them and offered a halfhearted greeting before asking them, without any further adieu, if they wanted to battle. We knew we would take them, and were dying to show the world. But they refused, trying their best to ignore us. We began to taunt: "Come on . . . Real quick . . . You scared?" hoping to pressure them into it; but still they ignored us. Realizing that they would not be swayed we finally left them alone and continued on to the hotel, now aware that Salt-N-Pepa would certainly be staying there.

By the time we arrived on the scene at the hotel, the crowd had already established itself around the front door, where it was held at bay by a single oversized security guard who was allowing no one past him without a hotel key. We walked straight to the front of the crowd like we belonged there and began to work on him. "We're part of the show!" we stressed to him, seeming perplexed by his refusal to believe us. To prove our point we burst out into a full-fledged rhyme production with Mouse on the beatbox. Everybody started jamming to our flow and the security guard started to believe us. We cemented the whole deal by showing him our COMPLIMENTARY tickets. That was it. We were in. As we walked over to the elevators there were some other folks waiting who looked as though they were with the production, so we followed. When they got off at the fourth floor we exited as well, and knew immediately that it was the right decision. As we stepped off the elevator there was a bodyguard that Tupac and Mouse knew from around the way. He asked us how we got in and we told him. He just laughed.

In the hallway there were random people milling about. At the end of the hall was Heavy D, sitting in a chair, relaxing. We headed toward him. Tupac walked up and engaged him casually, politely asking for any words of advice for young brothers trying to break into the business. Heavy looked exhausted behind his dark sunglasses, but was extremely cool nonetheless, offering us but a quick word: simply, "You gotta pay your dues."

Walking away from Heavy we were ready for the main course, an audience with Salt-N-Pepa. To achieve this we employed the assistance of Tupac and Mouse's security guard friend. We returned to him and asked that he please go into the room where they were chilling and ask them to come out to speak to us for just a minute. Understandably he was reluctant, but eventually he gave way to our insistence. When he walked back out of the room, Salt stuck her head out behind him, and with a sorrowful expression told us that they weren't signing any autographs at that time.

"No, no," we answered quickly, "we want you to hear us for a minute. We're a group." She was reluctant but allowed us to talk her into giving us just a minute. Here it was. We were there. The perfect story of discovery. This was where it was going to happen. We were going to knock her off her feet with talent and energy.

"Alright, y'all ready," Tupac said, looking to us, and then specifically to Mouse. Time seemed almost to stand still. The bell of the elevator sounded daintily in the background. Mouse drew in his breath to begin, but before he could get out a sound:

"Hey! I knew y'all didn't belong in here." It was the security guard from the front door. He came walking speedily toward us, repeating himself: "I knew y'all didn't belong in here. Come on!" he said waving to us to come to him.

"Hold on just one second," we all said to him in unison. "She's giving us a second."

"Naw, come on!" he refused, reaching us and herding us away, ignoring our pleas. Salt gave him no sanction to do this to us, but neither did she intervene on our behalf. We were in shock. We couldn't believe it. So close we had gotten, and so far we had come, only for it all to be snatched away by this idiot!

On the elevator we let it all out, digging into him, deep: cursing, cracking on him, talking about his mother, just bludgeoning him with words. "I guess mawfuckas don't have *DREAMS*! Like us! That's why you're a security guard! You ever had a dream?! You ever wanna *be* somethin' in life?!" Tupac in particular was just going at him with reckless abandon, psychologically even. It would have been much funnier if not within the context of so tragic an occurrence.

We exited the elevator still on the security guard's case, giving him a few parting words before heading through the lobby to the front door. But on our way, hope again exploded within. Herbie Lovebug (Salt-N-Pepa's producer) came walking through the door with an associate. Without a second thought we walked straight up to him and offered a confident greeting.

"Do you listen to new groups?" we asked.

"I don't listen to tapes," he replied, "I listen to groups live," thinking that this would intimidate us and catch us off guard. But this was perfect. We hadn't any tape. "Live" was what we were all about, and we answered as much, asking for a quick minute.

"Alright man," he replied gruffly, taking a look at his watch and then settling into an observational posture, looking back to us. Here we were again: another incredible chance, and this time we were going to *kill it*!

We shifted our weight and adjusted our posture, positioning ourselves toward him. Just as we had planned to do with Salt, we were going to bust out with our joint, "Check It Out," an excellent showcase of our tight collaborative flow. Again Mouse drew in a breath, expanding his chest.

"Naw, I ain't got time for this shit!" Herbie Lovebug burst out, out of nowhere, with no hint of sensitivity or remorse. "I gotta be on a plane in ten hours," he added with a drawl, again looking down to his watch and walking off without another word. We stood there frozen, with our mouths open, truly in shock this time. It was over. Our big chance had come and gone.

Right then and there we each took out our ticket stubs, held them in the air, and pledged: "Whoever is the first to make it, *Dis!* that motherfucker!" In my first conversation with Tupac after he had left Baltimore, and after his role in *Juice* and his work with Digital Underground, one of the first things he said to me was, "Darrin, I got him." I didn't understand what he meant until he explained how Herbie Lovebug had approached him at the opening of the movie *Juice* and expressed a desire to work with him. Tupac had employed no restraint in his scathing, immediate reply. We enjoyed a good, prolonged laugh at this one.

. . .

September was fast approaching and I still didn't have the money for school. Everything was set for me to attend the School of Visual Arts (SVA) in New York except for my tuition. Unsuccessfully, I scrambled about, looking for money through scholarships, financial aid, loans, whatever. When I was worn out from the stress of it all, my grandmother let me know that she would come up with the remaining money. It would be extremely difficult, but she told me she would do it. Right at this same time, I won the 1988 Baltimore NAACP-ACTSO competition for photography, drawing, and sculpture. I then went on to the national competition, where I took home the second place prize for sculpture. In total I won a cash prize of two thousand five hundred dollars. Tupac was ecstatic, almost happier for me than I was for myself. He held such a profound respect for successful achievement, and performance at the highest levels, that for someone in his inner circle, his closest crew, to experience such success was reason for great celebration and acknowledgment. Without delay he took me to his mother's apartment so that he could tell her what I had achieved. He filled her in with such enthusiasm, it was like he had won himself. Ms. Shakur was also very impressed, and sat me down for another one of those serious and inspiring talks, urging me to push forward with bravery, vision, and unbreakable resolve. Most of my prize money I earmarked for school. But with a good chunk of it, eight hundred dollars, I purchased a Roland drum machine for the group, so that we could make some real, original beats for our songs.

But this period of good fortune and positive momentum did not last for very long. Around this same time, not too long after the

Salt-N-Pepa show, we students of the School for the Arts were stricken by a horrible tragedy. Isha Moses, one of the best-liked girls in the school, and the girl I had adored and loved from afar since the very first day she set foot in the school, was killed in an automobile accident. Isha was an unusually kind soul who I don't think had a beef with anyone in the school. And I had not only been enamored with her, but had been an extremely close friend, so the loss was particularly hard on me. For a long time afterward I was changed in a fundamental way; at times I was practically comatose. As soon as I found out about the accident and Isha's death, I found myself writing a long poem about all that her life meant to me and to the world around her. It was as if I entered a trance and the poem just gushed forth from some unconscious source, communicating my feelings exactly. I planned to ask her mother if I could read it at the funeral. I read it to Tupac over the phone, and I could hear in his reaction that he was blown away. "Damn, you wrote that?!" he asked. He immediately went about writing one himself. The next day, over at Gerard's, he pulled a folded piece of notebook paper out of his pocket and told me that he wanted me to hear something, that he had also written a poem for Isha. I was mortified as he read it to me. The context in which he wrote the poem didn't make sense at all. He didn't know her like I did. And he didn't love her like I did. This was just about him wanting to write something better than me. I think he even had some vision of us combining the poems into a song and performing them, verse for verse, at the funeral. Who knows? Anyway, the poem he wrote just wasn't sincere and he knew it. He knew that I knew it as well. It was full of all of this inflated emotion and deeply personal sentiment that I knew he didn't really feel: How could he? He didn't know her like that. As good an actor as he was, he did a terrible job of convincing me that day. Before he even finished, he did something I had never seen him do before. He stopped reading and was like, "That's aright," and just balled the paper up and threw it in a nearby trash can. He knew it wasn't real. And he saw that I wasn't going to attempt to convince him otherwise.

I really think he was struck by my poem, by its handling of something so complex and ambiguous as death. I had never heard him deal with death in any of his rhymes before except for the rhyme he wrote for Darren Barrett. I think this was one instance in which he saw me on another level of poetry, as I generally saw him. My poem expressed feeling that could not be faked. And he had tried to fake it, and had failed miserably. His balling up the poem and throwing it away shocked me. I almost felt bad for him, and told him, "Yeah, that was aright." While really, I was glad he had seen the truth for himself, and had taken the initiative to deal with the poem as it deserved to be dealt with.

After the funeral, a mutual friend of Tupac's and mine told me that he made an incredibly insensitive statement in the car on the way home from the service. She told me that he said to her and everyone in the car, "She was the only girl I ain't get," referring to Isha. What a disgusting statement! I didn't call him on it. In fact, I never approached him about it. It was too sore a subject for me. His confidence had boiled over into arrogance this time. All I could think was, "So what you fucked the whole school! Now, I'm not fucking impressed. Now you're fucking arrogant. Grow the fuck up." It always had to be about Tupac. But it wasn't about Tupac this time. It was about the most beautiful girl I had ever known being cut down in the prime of her life. And he couldn't be humble for just one fucking minute. I was disgusted. Yet at the same time, I knew how he just said shit out his mouth without thinking. I'm sure he had no idea exactly how disgusting his statement was. He most certainly knew not to say those remarks around me for he knew it would have surely triggered something awful in me. I neither saw nor spoke to him for over two weeks. I'm not even sure if he knew something was wrong.

Then one night I saw him on TV, on the news. He was being interviewed by a reporter from one of the local news programs who was out in the neighborhood, getting the opinion of residents on the Saturday Night Specials controversy. Back in the day, Saturday Night Specials were cheaply made, widely distributed little handguns that were as easy to obtain as a loaf of bread. His in-depth familiarity with these guns was astounding to me. I had no idea. He went on and on about the guns, talking about how hazardous they were because they were so cheaply and so poorly made. Comfortably, he got into the intricacies so that the reporter himself was a little taken aback. I guess in his Black Panther upbringing he had an unusual technical familiarity with firearms.

Seeing him on TV made me smile; I called him up. I told him that I had seen him on the news and we eased into a comfortable conversation. I didn't say anything about the comment. I wasn't interested in hearing it, or bringing it up for discussion. After this conversation we didn't speak again until I called him right before leaving for New York. I was still upset, still a little standoffish. In addition to everything, I could kind of feel that things were coming to an end, that we were going our separate ways. Despite my optimistic high hopes for what I might accomplish for the group in New York, it being the very center of the hip-hop industry, the contacts I might establish, the reality of the distance that would separate us was daunting, and the conversation was strained. He was obviously uncomfortable with the fact that I had graduated and was leaving town. And he allowed this to manifest outwardly in the form of a subtle curtness. He closed the conversation with an ominous revelation, told with the typical Tupac bluntness. With genuine alarm, he told me, "Darrin, be careful. I had a dream you went up to New York and got shot."

 **He Made It**

When I returned home from school for the holidays in December of 1988, Tupac was nowhere to be found. No one could tell me exactly what had happened to him, or where he had gone. There was only vague mention of some "area" of California. He, Ms. Shakur, and Setchua had left Baltimore in a hurry, and apparently under some kind of duress while I was still in New York. I remembered him mentioning a possible move out to California to his aunt's house, so I figured this was where they must have gone.

For two years I heard nothing until around the time he landed the role in *Juice*. We reestablished contact through Jada, who told me he was trying to get in touch with me. She was also in California, pursuing her acting career, and had been in touch with him. She gave me his number. When he and I talked soon after, he eagerly filled me in on all of the events of the past two years, how he had just done a movie, and all of the people he had met in the business. Of course he was particularly proud of a couple of young stars he had slept with. He asked about my grandmother and the rest of my family, my artwork, and other friends such as Gerard and his parents. I filled him in as best I could. After this initial conversation we corresponded infrequently. It would be a number of years before we would see each other again.

In '91 Tupac returned to Baltimore for a brief visit, making his rounds, visiting the school, friends, etc. He and John stopped by my grandmother's house; a couple of my neighbors raced to tell me when I arrived only a few minutes afterward, but no one had been home for him to leave a message. I would not see him before his flight out of Baltimore the next day. Within a week Mouse flew out to California and John and I made plans to join them. I spoke with Tupac and Mouse over the phone on several occasions. Tupac told me to come on out, running down what it was like to live out there. "Darrin, I can tell you about anybody you want to know about," he told me, conveying exactly how deeply he was in the mix of the music and movie industries. I got pumped. I would drive out with John in a few months, after we had a chance to get all of our affairs in order. But as the scheduled day of departure approached, I changed my mind. I knew that I had my own life to lead and couldn't well do it following Tupac.

A couple years, two albums, and another major film later, Mouse was back in Baltimore after a serious falling out with Tupac; John had long since returned. It was 1993. I heard that Tupac was going to be performing at Hammer Jacks down below the harbor and decided that I was going to see him. The night of the show I caught a cab down to the club with no plan or prior contact. When I approached the building the Baltimore radio personality promoting the event, Frank Ski, was out in front. I asked him to please do me a favor, that a very good personal friend of mine was performing there that night and to please tell him, "Darrin will be out by the stage." He said that he would. When I saw him inside shortly thereafter he told me that he delivered the message and that Tupac was looking for me. Unsure of what to expect, I hung out by the front of the stage and waited.

After an hour or so the opening act finished and Frank Ski reappeared on stage. Pumping up the crowd for Tupac's entrance he enthusiastically introduced the now popular rapper as "Mr. I Get Around," a reference to his current hit single. To this the crowd went wild with loud cheering and applause. As soon as Tupac came into view the noise erupted anew. Immediately, he spotted me off to the corner and walked directly to me, embracing me with a big hug and even taking a minute to talk. Meanwhile the whole place waited, cheering. Before he continued onto the stage he stressed to me, "We gotta kick it after the show." It felt good. He had put on no airs, and had, without reservation, given me my due props.

After the show we hung out backstage in his dressing room, bullshittin' with everyone there and dealing with the hordes of those attempting to get back to see him. Distressed by the chaos, he told his bodyguards not to let anyone else back. "*This* is my homie," he said pointing to me. "Fuck everybody else!"

I felt honored by the statement, and the seriousness with which he delivered it. But at the same time, the words pierced me in a painful way. The main person that was at the door trying to see him was Herb, from the School for the Arts. I don't know why he dissed Herb like that, but I guess he had his reasons.

After leaving Hammer Jacks I rode with Tupac and some of the crew in their rented minivan back to his hotel room at the Days Inn in downtown Baltimore. Once in the room he lit up a joint and we began to smoke, easing into our trip back down memory lane. All the while there was chaos: groupies in almost nothing, standing around hoping to get chosen; guys crowding around with tapes, hoping for a break. But we paid them no mind; we had a lot of catching up to do. Tupac was seated on the edge of the window and I on his bed. As he always did when I hadn't spoken with him for an extended period, he asked about my grandmother, and then about Gerard and his parents. "I remember you ain't let *nobody* say *nothin'* about your grandmom boy," he joked; he remembered. It was almost surreal. Such a close friend whom I had known so intimately, and then watched awkwardly through the media for so many years. And now, once again we were together, kickin' it just like old times, just like nothing had changed. And in many ways nothing had; he hadn't changed a bit. He possessed the same character, the same demeanor. I was shocked by the way he remembered everything, all of the little details that I was certain he hadn't given a second thought about after leaving Baltimore. He told me that his mom asked about me, and proceeded to give me the rundown of the family: Scott and Kenny were okay and in New York, and had also asked about me.

After colorfully repainting our School for the Arts days in great detail and depth, we discussed more current subjects, delving into industry-related topics.

I was amazed by all of the opportunity he was being presented with, and the caliber of people with which he was coming into contact. He told me about Janet Jackson, and how he had tried to get John to do a painting of her on a horse for her birthday. "So fucking simple!" he exclaimed, still visibly vexed. "Janet on a horse! But nooo . . ." Apparently John had insisted on doing something totally different, something that Tupac wasn't feeling at all. So the gift was never extended. I told him that he should have called me and asked me to do it.

We talked about many of the different rap stars and how he felt that most were shockingly phony. In particular he berated those from the east coast. "I have nothing against the east coast . . . I'm *from* the east coast . . . I *love* the east coast," he told me. "But a lot of these rappers ain't real . . . They not fuckin' real!" he continued, going on to tell me how east coast rappers were all into "style," how everything was about "style," with no consideration for what was real and true in their lives. He felt these rappers were largely acting, inflating the lives of others. "They talk about guns, and they talk all this shit . . . But they not doin' shit! When I came to California I started to see that muthafuckas wasn't just talkin' shit, they was doin' it!" He told me that it was when he saw a Mexican cat raise up through the sunroof of a little bug and start spraying a whole street corner in broad daylight that he realized, "These muthafuckas out here ain't playin'." In stark contrast to this hard reality into which he was thrown upon his arrival in Marin City, and in which he had been raised in New York and Baltimore, was an unmistakable scarcity of true, unadulterated heart among those in the industry. He witnessed a disturbing portrayal of hardness presented theatrically to the public while the reality, seen firsthand by himself, was one of softness and uselessness under pressure.

We talked until six in the morning. At times it seemed like he completely forgot about the bullshit that had in so many ways become his life, re-entering the innocent body of his seventeen-year-old self and transplanting himself back into those days so many years before. At one point in the conversation I told him that people were going to look at him in a prophetic way, that I could see that kind of energy in his life, growing out of the extraordinary energy of his mother. He just smiled and replied humbly, "Darrin, I was homeless . . . I didn't know *what* I was gonna do." This kind of shocked me because I hadn't really known about all of the hardship he originally endured out in California. I had assumed his transition to the new area, and his subsequent ascent to his current icon status, were both smooth and storylike. I wasn't aware of the gritty details.

When the evening finally wound down, I ended up crashing there on the floor while he took the bed. A couple hours later we were abruptly awakened by his manager, who banged on the door. Only after it was obvious he would not go away did I defy Tupac's orders, delivered angrily from beneath the covers, and open the door. Visibly upset at my slow reaction, the manager barged into the room and informed us that they were all being thrown out of the hotel for making too much noise the night before. Tupac was incensed, and demanded to know why he was being so inconvenienced when all he had done all night was sit in his room and talk to his homeboy. "*Y'all* must uh been fuckin' up! *Y'all* leave! *I'm* stayin'! *I* ain't do shit! . . . I ain't do shit!" he kept repeating adamantly.

After all of his things had been packed and he came downstairs into the hotel lobby, he was still highly upset, and demanded to speak to the manager of the hotel. "I'm not gonna hit'm or nothin'. I just wanna see'm," he told the personnel behind the front desk, almost yelling. "I want him to tell me, man to man, why I'm being thrown out." Needless to say the manager never showed his/her face.

Abandoning his offensive, he walked with me over toward the front of the lobby. I looked him in the eye: "So what's up? Are we gonna do this this time or what?" Everyone was waiting for him on the bus. As Born Busy we had dreamed of bursting onto the music scene as a group. He and I had been family, through an extremely impressionable and precious stage of our development into the men that we had become. I felt comfortable asserting that his family of people around him was not complete without me.

"It's hard work," he replied. I told him that I understood full well, that there was nothing for me in Baltimore anymore, and that I would even work for free if need be. "Arright man," he said. "Give me five minutes."

Leaving me in the lobby, he walked over to the bus and boarded. After a couple minutes his manager emerged from the front door and waved me over. When I boarded everyone began to cheer. Everyone, that is, except the manager who took in my presence through contracted eyes behind a belabored smile. Those close to the front patted me on the back and offered kind words. Then Tupac spoke up, initiating the vote required from all on board. They unanimously voted me in. I was going to join him.

I immediately began to give away all of my things, and to bid my farewells to friends and family in order to leave in three days as they had said; but it was not to be. Two days later I received a phone call from the manager telling me that there were conflicts in the contract with the record company prohibiting me from joining the tour at that time. We set a later date for the next quarter when a new contract would be drawn up, but I never spoke with Tupac directly, and received only the cold shoulder from the manager. I made no attempt to rectify the situation. A few months later I received a message from Tupac through a mutual friend who ran into him. Simply, "We gotta go," was the message he instructed the friend to give me.

He still knew who I was, as one of the few trues who had always been real with him and there for him whenever it came down to it. And he wanted me to know this. But I realized it was not meant to be, and over the next few years in Baltimore I would see exactly why. My life headed in a very different direction from that which it certainly would have taken on tour with them. And the growth I underwent during this period is undoubtedly my greatest treasure, largely responsible for my ability to take on this project in a way that I feel no one else could.

Epilogue

The journey on which I set out to complete this project has now come to a place of closure. A new chapter in my life follows the last chapter of this book. For me, the journey has been a very spiritual one. And it has been a certain spiritual commitment that I have felt that has driven me through this incredibly difficult, drawn-out endeavor from beginning to end.

When I look back through the pages of this story, I smile because I know that I did my very best to paint a picture of the Tupac I knew so well through our years together in high school. And when I think of the great opportunity afforded me through the publishing of this work, I can't help but remember all that it took to get here. It has been some journey: one in which I could not possibly have been successful without a great deal of help. This help has come from many different people, as I expressed in my acknowledgments, and, I unapologetically maintain, from forces and energies that lie beyond the realm of people.

Regardless of the number of books written about Tupac in the years following his death, I always knew that my story about this incredible personality was unique, and necessary. But I initially doubted my ability to complete such an ambitious undertaking. I remember clearly, lying in bed on the eve of my deciding, once and for all, to take on this project, having been tormented for weeks by vivid dreams and haunting waking thoughts of my old friend. I called out to his spirit, and asked that if he wished for me to assume the challenge of telling his story, to please let me know for certain, to give me a sign.

Early the next morning I awoke to get some old photographs of him notarized. Having visited, unsuccessfully, three notary offices that were closed, I decided to make one last attempt. When I arrived at the office of the notary up the street from my grandmother's house on Rogers Avenue, Mr. Rice, the neighborhood taxman and notary, was walking through the door. He notarized the photographs and I told him that they were of Tupac Shakur. To this he replied with particular interest, telling me that his daughter was a writer who had recently written a magazine article on Tupac. I was shocked. Right at that moment his daughter came into the office. After a quick introduction I asked her what it was that she had written about Tupac. Without hesitation she produced the piece from her briefcase.

All of a sudden there I was standing in the one notary public office open at that early hour, holding a published article on Tupac (with a blown-up picture of him on the front) and having a heart-to-heart with the author. We were engaged in a relatively heated discussion. Although written beautifully, the article failed to go any further than what had already been widely reported by the mass media (some information true, some not). I disagreed with some of what she had written, but I respected her intentions and enjoyed our conversation. Right then and there I knew that Tupac had communicated with me, and that this book was a responsibility from which I could not back down. There would be a succession of such curiously coincidental events throughout my effort that were as responsible for what you have read as any other contributing factor.

In the initial days of my journey through this project I spent a great deal of time in the Enoch Pratt Free Library in downtown Baltimore, reading old newspaper articles, visiting Web sites dedicated to Tupac, and researching up-and-coming projects pertaining to him. The feeling of many people who knew of my commitment to this project was that it was a waste, that the same was certainly being done already, many times over. So I wanted to see exactly what *was* being done. As I expected, I found nothing more than further exploitation of the already well known, sadly skewed story of the larger than life, tragically out of control, celebrity for whom no one dared venture a guess toward his deeper thoughts and motivations, toward the intricately complex young man behind the myth. I was reaffirmed in the dire need for this book and saw, more and more, exactly why I should take on the project.

When I casually mentioned the project to a librarian I had noticed on each of my previous visits, he told me that Tupac had won a library-sponsored contest there, and that the woman who presided over the event was still there. I remembered Tupac telling me of such a contest, so I was very excited, and interested in meeting her. Within minutes I found myself speaking with Deborah Taylor, Director of Youth Services, who remembered the contest and Tupac's group vividly, having given them a ride to the event since they had none otherwise. Happy to finally see someone interested in addressing the Tupac that she remembered, she pledged her full support and provided me with his and Mouse's entry submission to the contest, handwritten by Tupac at age fourteen, along with other very useful details from the experience. Ms. Taylor had been genuinely impressed with the fourteen-year-old Tupac, and sincerely interested in the megastar he eventually became, so she was happy to assist someone who wished to explore the young man that she knew and respected. It is interesting to note that the above-mentioned written submission is now on display in the archives of the Enoch Pratt Library alongside the work of such famous Baltimore artists as Edgar Allan Poe.

Throughout this process I have been shocked by not only the unbelievably diverse cross-section of society that was interested in Tupac, but the extent to which so many of these people were affected by him in his few years on the national stage. Like the next-door neighbor of a girlfriend I stayed with in the first year of my research and writing effort. He played Tupac's music *all the time*, nonstop, and loud, *very* loud. He must have been the biggest Tupac fan I ever encountered. One minute he was on the front porch with a buddy of his talking and cranking Tupac, and the next minute he was on the back porch talking to his boys on the phone, *still* playing Tupac. His conversations, also much louder than they needed to be, were also concerning Tupac and all of Tupac's lyrics. It was as if this guy was the leader of some sort of study group focused on the philosophies of Tupac. He was always home and he was always playing and discussing Tupac.

For two months this went on without interruption, until it became more annoying than I could bear. The irony was just too thick to be of mere coincidence, and I began to envision Tupac's spirit tickled silly by the sick humor of the whole affair, looking down on me laughing heartily. I decided it was time to go next door and give this guy the biggest shock of his life. As usual he was out on the front porch listening to Tupac—loud, this time with two of his boys. When I walked up to them and got a closer look, I saw that the guy was at least thirty years old, and that he was an exceptionally big and intimidating fellow. I asked him if he wanted to see something and he said, "Sure." I showed him a photograph of Tupac at age seventeen taken in Baltimore. He was shocked. I then played for them the tape that Gerard had given me, the recording of us as Born Busy back in 1988; their undivided attention was mine. When I asked the guy what it was he wanted to know about Tupac, he asked me questions pertaining to exactly the issues and topics that I was addressing in the book, still in its early stages of development. This reaffirmed my confidence that I was on the right track. He then went on to tell me a funny story of how he had a near run-in with Tupac back in the day. Apparently his friends, dishwashers, had asked him to come down to their job at the Market Place restaurant to help them out with a beef they were having with this kid (Tupac) and his friend. I couldn't believe it; I immediately busted out laughing and told him, "I was the friend!" I then recapped the entire scenario for him. We tripped about this into the evening. There was no doubt in my mind that Tupac's spirit was laughing along with me at this hilarious turn of events. Looking at the guy, I couldn't help but acknowledge how lucky it had been for us that he had had something else to do that day nine years before.

Everywhere I went it seemed that Tupac followed. At one point about a year into the effort it got to be too much. I felt consumed by the story. It was as if I could do nothing else. Everywhere I turned there was someone or something else involving the story. I couldn't escape. I had no money and I was neither eating nor sleeping properly. I was frustrated and completely burned out, having put my entire life on hold. Feeling that I might be slowly losing my sanity, I began to question whether it was all worth it. I even began to ask Tupac to please just give me a break!

Looking for emotional support, I went to Truxon Sykes, who had become my principal mentor, and conveyed to him my extreme exhaustion. I told him that the pressure was getting to be too much, and that I wanted to say "Forget it!" to the whole thing. He told me that Tupac was counting on me, and that I had to find the strength, from somewhere, to follow this thing through to completion. He also told me that I needed to stop looking at this as some kind of curse, that I was actually being provided a great opportunity, not only to share an important part of Tupac's life with the world, but to pursue some of my own grandest dreams. This all sounded beautiful and inspiring, but it in no way resolved the fact that I was painfully fatigued and in desperate need of a long break, far away from the project.

I left Truxon's and walked over to my uncle's house nearby. After a short visit he offered me a ride home, but, strangely, I turned it down, deciding rather to take the bus; it was eleven P.M. The bus came and left but I remained on the stop. I found myself walking toward the old house on Greenmount Avenue where Tupac had stayed with his sister and mother in the first floor apartment; it was only four blocks away. To get to the house I walked straight down Greenmount Avenue (definitely not recommended at that time of night). When I arrived at the home I asked a girl sitting on the stoop next door in which building had Tupac lived, just to make sure. She pointed to the house in front of me, reaffirming what I had remembered. The building was vacant at the time and there were green plastic bags taped to the windows. I made a mental note to return to take pictures, and then proceeded down to Greenmount and 33rd, where I would, hopefully, catch a bus that would get me to the subway in time for the last train going uptown.

Arriving at the subway station in time, I found only one other brother in the whole place. He was walking in front of me down the escalator. When we got down to the platform at the level of the tracks I stopped and sat on the edge of the escalators while he kept walking to the first bench, on which I noticed a pile of newspaper. He stopped at the bench and picked up the newspaper. Watching him look through it, I sensed that that paper had something to do with Tupac. I didn't know why, I just had a strong feeling. The guy then put the paper down and continued toward the end of the platform, stopping at the second bench. I then got up and walked over to the bench and sat down. I took out Truxon's book, *The Principles of the Body Universe*, and began to read, periodically taking long looks at the paper beside me. When the last downtown train arrived in the station the breeze that accompanied it blew the paper on to the uptown track in front of me. The entire paper was blown onto the tracks except for one sheet which remained on the bench. I put the book away and picked up the remaining sheet. The first article on which I focused was an interview with Jasmine Guy. In it she was discussing her career. The author then went on to explain how she had recently lost a close friend of hers, rapper Tupac Shakur. She talked about how she had frequently complained to her now deceased friend about her career, to which he would quickly reply, "Girl please . . . Just get off your ass and do it!" Chills shot through my body as I read this statement; I heard Tupac's voice ringing in my head, telling me, "Just get off your ass and do it!"

As soon as I got to my destination, Rogers Avenue subway

station, I called Truxon and told him what had happened. "I told you that Tupac wants you to finish this book," he replied. "And he's telling you to get off of your ass and do it!" That evening reinvigorated me, and I would not falter again, no matter how difficult things got.

A month later I found myself on a plane to California. I had been in touch with John Singleton's publicist in L.A., whom I had met through Mouse. After trying long and hard she finally convinced me to come out to L.A. in order to partner with her on a film project about the story I was writing. I had never been to California before, and had no idea what to expect.

While I perused some of the material I had written, an attractive young lady in her mid-twenties who was seated beside me began to make conversation. When I told her I was writing a book about my teenage experiences with Tupac Shakur, her eyes lit up and a big smile spread over her face. "The rapper, Tupac?" she asked. She then shot her right hand in the air and swore she was one of his biggest fans. She even kept a huge poster of him in her bedroom, directly over her bed, despite feeling that she was far too old to do such a thing. She said there were two things in life that she loved: teddy bears and Tupac. There was no other way to put it, she told me, "I'm absolutely in love with Tupac!" Then came the inevitable question, "Do you think he is still alive, or dead?" I told her that Tupac was very much alive in spirit, and that his spiritual presence had been a continuing source of strength and guidance for me over the course of my journey through this project. Although I could give her no concrete, firsthand confirmation, I told her that I believed he existed no longer in the physical. I took my reply very seriously, and tried to be as compassionate as I possibly could because I could sense how much Tupac meant to her. Immediately her eyes began to water. And after a couple of seconds she could hold it in no longer, and burst out in a full-fledged fit of sobbing right there in front of me. She could hardly believe what I had told her. I could feel the other passengers looking at us, wondering why this pretty young woman was now crying like she was, so I attempted to console her and make her feel better. Even though deep inside she knew the shooting in Las Vegas was no hoax, it was just so hard for her to come to grips with the idea that Tupac was no longer around: He would never write another song, do another interview, make another video. The rest of the trip I thought long and hard about exactly how deeply Tupac affected millions of people around the world. And I felt bad about being the one to crush so strong a fleeting hope in so beautiful a person as this young woman. I was the closest link to Tupac she had ever had, and she immediately accepted what I told her as fact.

I talked to many people about Tupac in my travels through the five years or so that it took me to complete this book. I found in every one a different story about how Tupac touched them. Their experience of him was never the same as mine. Yet each and every one led me to reflect, a little differently each time, on my own experience with Tupac and how he affected and continues to affect me. I came to realize that this book actually saved my life.

When I returned home to Baltimore over three years later, I returned with a fresh new perspective on life. For years, before embarking on this journey, I felt uninspired and unsure about pursuing my artistic talents. I was unable to envision myself reaching an audience on the scale that I felt was necessary, and consequently wondered, "What's the point?" Something was eating at me, and I didn't know what it was. What I'm now certain of was a formidable case of depression led me to make excuses for myself in the face of

my consistent failure to finish what I started, whether it be a work
of art or business idea. I was content with knowing that my life had
taken the path of an artist, instead of actually being the artist as I
envisioned and barreling through a select plethora of ideas always
floating about in my mind to some finished product that would
speak for itself. I felt like I was losing my mind as well as wasting
the very talent that made me who I am. I would even complain
of how Baltimore didn't have many outlets or venues for creative
people. I needed to believe that my life's efforts on this planet
would bring me more joy than what I was witnessing from others
that were content with their routine lives. I knew through all the
pain that I was enduring within myself that living toward my destiny was up to me. I just didn't internalize it anymore.

Unable to finish anything I started, and unable to find anything
that would make a difference, I just shut down, and discontinued
my art all together. But since persevering through the many stages
of this book, not so easily allowing the vision to blur, and continuing forward out of responsibility to Tupac whenever it did, I have
been inspired anew, even reborn as an artist. This book has been
wonderful medicine for me as it allowed me to make a difference in
people's understanding of Tupac, provoking them to think a little
more deeply about him, eliciting from them an emotional response,
which is most satisfying and invigorating to me as an artist. The
memories in this book reintroduced lessons to me that I was able to
draw from and apply to the current phase of my life. In revisiting
this period of my life I have been able to reclaim those lessons in
successful attainment learned from Tupac in our years together.
No matter the circumstance, Tupac would never surrender his self-
confidence and his vision, as I had in so many instances. He would
hold tightly to these through whatever storm might arise, and he

would use them to persevere. This valuable lesson I have reclaimed, and shall never lose again.

My primary objective for this book has always been to allow the world to take another look at Tupac, through my eyes, at a time in his life when he was discovering who he was and what he was capable of becoming. If those who have read this book have felt the power of Tupac's dream, the incredible strength of his fortitude, and the depth of his love for humankind, then I have remained true to my responsibility to my friend.

DATE DUE

BRODART, CO.

Cat. No. 23-221-003